SATOSHI'S VISION

The Art of Bitcoin

Craig Wright

Satoshi's Vision ©2019 by Craig Wright.
All rights reserved. No part of this book may be reproduced in any form or by any electronic or mechanical means including information storage and retrieval systems, without permission in writing from the author. The only exception is by a reviewer, who may quote short excerpts in a review.

Interviews and Compilation by Paul Democritou
Edited by Sandra Seymour

The opinions expressed in this book are those of the author or speaker and do not reflect the opinions of Howson Books, it's editors or affiliates. Neither Howson Books nor its authors or editors guarantees the accuracy or completeness of any information published herein. Howson Books, it's authors and editors shall not be responsible for any errors, omissions, or claims for damages, including exemplary damages, arising out of use, inability to use, or with regard to the accuracy or sufficiency of the information contained in this publication.
Nothing in this book constitutes legal, financial, or other professional advice. Information contained herein is current as of the date of publication to the best knowledge of Howson Books, its editors and authors.

Craig Wright
Visit my website at https://craigwright.net/

First Printing: August 2019

Howson Books
HowsonBooks.com

CONTENTS

Foreword 1

Being Satoshi 3
    I am Satoshi 4
    Freedom of Speech Versus Privacy 32
    The Burden of Proof 38

Bitcoin Vision 50
    What is Bitcoin? 51
    Peer-To-Peer 57
    Digital Cash 60
    Scalability 67
    Security 69
    Stability 74

Dispelling the Myths 76
    What Bitcoin is Not 77
    Code is Not Law 78
    It is Not Anonymous 81
    Pseudonimity 85
    It's Not Anarchist 91
    It's Not Socialist 92
    It's Not For Crime 97
    Core is Not Bitcoin 102
    Cash is Not Bitcoin 108

Correcting Mistakes 118
    There Can Be Only One 119
    Fixing the Protocol 128
    Ensuring Stability 132
The Road Ahead 135
    The BSV Roapdmap 139
    The Long-Haul 149
    Acknowledgements 153

FOREWORD

LOVE HIM OR HATE HIM, YOU CAN'T IGNORE CRAIG WRIGHT. I had been interviewing some of the most influential people in the cryptocurrency industry for a little over a year when I first had the opportunity to speak with Craig.

Our first interview was conducted on video, for inclusion in the second edition of *The Crypto Factor* interviews book. But it quickly became obvious that to tell Craig's story, it would need a book of its own. Since then, I have conducted several more interviews with Craig, and used them, along with Craig's published blog posts and papers, to compile this book.

In *Satoshi's Vision: The Art of Bitcoin*, Craig explains how the pseudonymous persona of Satoshi Nakamoto came about, where the original idea of Bitcoin came from, and why he stepped down from public interaction. He talks frankly about his original vision, and how Bitcoin as we know it today differs from that, concluding with his plans to bring the original vision to fruition, and what that means for the future of Bitcoin.

I cannot say that I agree with Craig on everything. We have had some lively discussions. But despite his prickly public persona, I have always felt comfortable in expressing my opinion with Craig and have nothing but the utmost respect for him as a person, and an entrepreneur.

Craig has a vision. That vision may or may not square with your own vision of what Bitcoin is or should be. He has opinions that may differ from yours, and rarely holds back in expressing them where his life's work is concerned. Agree or disagree, you would be a fool not to listen to and understand Craig's arguments. Because Craig Wright is in the game for the long-haul. He expects establishing and perfecting Bitcoin to keep him busy for the next thirty years or more. By that time, he hopes you will be using his invention daily without even being aware of it, "like plumbing."

Craig also has some startling and controversial predictions for the future of cryptocurrency in general and Bitcoin in particular. While it may be said that only time will tell whether Craig's predictions will turn out to be true, or whether the market will lead in a different direction, those predictions are based on extensive knowledge and experience, and participators in the field ignore that at their peril.

I would encourage everyone already involved in the cryptocurrency industry or considering investing, developing, or working within it to read and consider Craig's opinions and beliefs, and to keep an open mind.

Paul Democritou

BEING SATOSHI

I AM SATOSHI

One of the first questions most people ask when they question me about being Satoshi Nakamoto is where the name came from, and what it means.

Satoshi Nakamoto is an amalgamation of 富永 仲基 (Tominaga Nakamoto) and Ash Ketchum (サトシ; Satoshi).

The name wasn't something that I spent months and months on deciding, and it doesn't mean anything related to what you see on the wikis. Rather, it was an attempt at privacy.

The Tokugawa period of Japan, between 1603 and 1868 was an interesting period of isolationism in the country. The opposite of what was happening in the West. Yet there was a monk who also talked about trade, and he wrote a lot. In his writings he talked about the need for open trade, open economy. The same sort of things that Adam Smith talked about, except in the wrong country at the wrong time. That was Tominga Nakamoto.

Ash is called Satoshi in Japan. It was a light-hearted reference to Ash the Pokémon trainer. I thought it was a good play on words, because The Economist had released a cover with a picture of a phoenix rising from the ashes, and they were talking about the rise of a single world currency. I thought it was funny. That Bitcoin would be the world currency, rising from the ashes.

There was a secondary part of the name Satoshi. Satoshi Sugiyama was adopted by an American and given the name David Phillips. It comes from a book, *The House of Morgan*. David was adopted in both cases. David Kleiman was adopted, and so was Satoshi. I admired the "characters" in the book. It reminded me of a more glorious and honourable period in banking. Not something that we could go back to, but something we could remember when formulating Bitcoin. Pierpoint Morgan was an interesting character and one who proved himself through work.

But at base, the moniker, Satoshi Nakamoto, was simply a way of being able to work and have some privacy in my life.

Next, people ask questions along the lines of, "Was Satoshi Nakamoto one person, or a group of people," and whether I wrote the original Bitcoin White Paper alone, or as part of a team effort.

The second question is easier to answer; I wrote the White Paper. There were some bits and pieces included which I had help with, and I had help with editing. But the White Paper is essentially my work. The matter of Satoshi being an individual or a group is a little more complex. Satoshi was a public persona I adopted, a part that I played. Yet even though I would say Satoshi was ninety percent me, other people helped, other people shaped the creation.

Invariably, people want to know why I felt the need for anonymity at the start. Why I dropped out of public sight, and why I chose to reappear and stake my claim to the Satoshi Nakamoto legacy after so many years away.

Put simply, I had concerns about the potential for illegal use of Bitcoin from the start, and the pseudonym was an attempt to put some distance between myself and that element. In the US, there are laws against the creation of software for the purposes of gaming. My concern was that these could be extended to money creation if the money created was then used for illegal purposes.

My past working as a prosecution forensic expert and in other roles with the government would not lead to a system that I could have publicly stood behind.

In order to fund my work, my partner Dave Kleiman and I sold code that was used in gaming out of countries such as Costa Rica. David took the biggest risk. Gambling is not illegal in Australia. But nothing Dave earned in Panama could be repatriated legally to the USA. On top of that, the mere issuing of coin was illegal. I wasn't American, but Dave was, so that was a problem.

All progress comes through a path of resistance. The cycle of revolt and revolution is one of change versus the status quo. With all technology, there is a rush forward and we take two steps. Then, as those who profited from the past start to see their world eroded, they push back and create a revolution.

I'm not proud of everything I have done. But I would do it again. I'm not always proud of the aggression and brashness and lack of polish I had in my past, but without them I would not be the man I am now. A part of me sought to resist change. The apotheosis into what I must become is not easy. And some of it involves owning my past and those things I've done to get to where I am now.

THE ROAD TO BITCOIN

I'd met Tim May back in the 80s when I was involved with DECUS under several SunOS groups. There were of course the black sheep groups such as the cypherpunks. But I understood that anarchy is a utopian pipedream.

Unfortunately, when you get groups of people who have little interaction with the real world, they start to believe stories and myths of a society that can exist without order. Worse, they start to believe in computerised order, the singularity, and that code is law. A few of us got on, but I was often ridiculed by people who refused to understand that risk is a probabilistic ideal and can never be perfected and removed. More importantly, I was ridiculed by people with no idea about how people or society work.

There is a lot to be said for a classical Western education.

I started formulating the idea back in the 90s. Unlike what people like Tim wanted, I wanted to make a money that wouldn't fall over because it was anonymous.

What has become Bitcoin and Metanet started in 1998 with a project I called Blacknet. It was never Tim May's version, BlackNet, although he was my inspiration for it. Tim and I were both aligned in being libertarian-Randian, but his concept was one of no government. He never saw that human nature has elements that would collapse it.

Tim had this idea of anonymous money that was going around. There were quite a number of them. Compact Cash, eCash, you could spin 20 different versions. The problem was, they all sought to be anonymous. And then they had this other problem. Tim thought everyone could have their own money, which is propagated through the cypherpunks.

That's the opposite of what money's about. The idea that everyone can print their own money, so, CraigCoin can go to Walmart, and WalmartCoin and CraigCoin can exchange. What is the use of everyone having their own currency? Or even multiples. The Euro is a great thing. It enables you to go around Europe without having to change your currency, like you used to. And that's only countries.

An anonymous cash type system will never work. Government can always just make it illegal. You know, government is the 800-pound gorilla, and you don't win by walking up to the gorilla and kicking it in the nuts. It might hurt it for a little bit. And then it rips your arms off and beats you with the bloody stubs.

Although I liked Tim, I knew in the 90s that I needed to find something else.

When I was working on Blacknet in 2005 and 2006, I stumbled upon what later became the solution to Bitcoin and the problems that I saw. DigiCash released eCash in the 1990s. It was a form of cryptocurrency that was more anonymous than Zcash or Monero, and it is nowhere to be found anymore. In part, the failure stemmed from an attack against the founding organisation, but eCash continued even after the bankruptcy of David Chaum's company. Creating a distributed group is not the solution people believe it to be. The problem is that they are not looking at the correct answer.

Many individuals acting in a distributed group on the same software program that is not a protocol that is fixed and immutable are in fact centralised. If we for instance take Zcash or Monero, or even Ethereum, every one of them comes back to a simple case of one organisation. Even where people say, "we are decentralised," they end in a single instance of an organisation. They neglect to note that they are under law an unlimited partnership.

Unfortunately, I have lost track of how much or little people know, especially when looking across disciplines. I have studied law, economics, computer science, history, mathematics, and even theology and ethics, and my greatest failure in doing so has been losing track of the understanding of the average person.

I did a master's degree in statistics to learn and understand propagation methodologies. During my studies I read a paper called "Ultrafast Consensus in Small-World Networks" (Olfati-Saber 2005). Following the discovery, I spent years going down the rabbit hole of Newman and Watts (Newman and Watts 1999). The node structure in Bitcoin is linked to the ledger.

Blacknet was a dead end not because it didn't work but because some of the earlier methodologies that are separate to Bitcoin now worked anonymously. An anonymous system will never be scaled to the world. At best, an anonymous system forms a methodology for black markets and illicit and illegal trade. I was never interested in creating a dark-web money.

I had staff back at DeMorgan, who didn't always even know what they were working on. They had tasks from me. Then for years I worked on ideas, going in circles. Not getting it right. I picked up a lot of ideas over the years. Not even everyone knows what part they played, to tell you the truth.

I was helped with some ideas from my grandfather. I was helped by Ellen Granger. I worked for an accounting firm, BDO, for a time, and that was one of the pieces of the puzzle of putting the idea together and getting it working finally. It proved the concept of the triple entry ledger. etc. I tried to do that with multiple distributed ways before but a network of competing entities attempting to find a ledger really came from an idea at accounting, because I was writing CAT software and doing forensic audits.

I know this seems a little bit strange for a few people, but Bitcoin started in its current iteration in 2007. That is when I knew that I could create the system that we have now.

In 2008, I studied law at the University of Northumbria, Newcastle. I completed an LLM in international commercial law and specialised in Internet intermediary liability. It was part of the key to Bitcoin. I needed to create a node system that allowed control yet freedom.

People fail to understand that Bitcoin is about balance and neutrality. A set protocol is one that allows online service providers (OSPs) to compete fairly in all the major jurisdictions globally. I have not considered North Korea. If you take the time to read the document that was my dissertation, (Wright 2008) you will note that I concluded that the simplest path was to restrict the end-state OSPs and hence the local jurisdictional node. In such a manner, individual governments can choose what they do and do not allow. Everything can be stored online, but not everyone can access it.

In the case of nodes, access is easily restricted, and ISPs can be required to filter certain types of access.

Personally, I do not like the idea of censoring open communication, but I do not believe in anonymous communications. It may, of course, seem ironic.

By the time Bitcoin was launched in January 2009, I had already dedicated over a decade of my life to it.

THE BIRTH OF BITCOIN

Few people understand what was required in the beginning of Bitcoin. It required a series of machines to send and transmit information without fail. This is far more difficult than you may imagine.

In my ranch that I used to own in Bagnoo, Australia, I converted part of my shed and home to run computers. In my house outside of Sydney, I took my garage and ran racks of machines.

I had racks of computers in my converted shed. With the mezzanine I had plenty of space. Earlier, I paid to have fibre laid and opened up a rural town to fast Internet.

The first version of Bitcoin following the genesis block fell over. The genesis block is dated 3rd January 2009. The first mined block occurred on 9th January. They are both days where I travelled to my farm. I had to travel 3 1/2 hours to get there.

I ran 67 machines in a cluster. They were Windows servers. I managed things and coded on Windows XP and loaded software on machines running on Windows Server 2003. The first version of Bitcoin was launched and started to run but stopped. There were program errors in the Bitcoin code, but they weren't the biggest problem. I needed to reconfigure the systems.

I'd started with a major miscalculation.

Microsoft patch Tuesday.

The original machines were a group of workstations and not a domain. When I initially installed them, I used a series of Windows Server 2003 licences. And then MS09-001.

It wasn't the first problem, but it was the biggest. All the machines weren't running at block one. There were what I hoped to be enough. Bitcoin didn't run on Linux at the time. I had Centos, Redhat, and Solaris machines on my network to handle DNS and sendmail, but Bitcoin ran on Windows.

The week between genesis and block one was busy. I moved away from Windows Server 2003 and set up a Windows 2008 domain. I set up a forest hierarchy with machines just outside of Sydney, in Bagnoo, and live links to a Melbourne server. I had connections to a Methodist Church just outside of California where I donated some time running their IT. I figured that since I paid for the systems sold, it wouldn't matter if I ran Bitcoin on the server. I did the same in Tumbi Umbi in the church there. Both had several machines that I'd set up. I paid for the Internet connections personally, and donated the servers and the licenses, so I figured using them to run Bitcoin nodes wasn't outside the scope of what I could do as it wasn't costing them anyway.

The first reboot was an eye opener. I had configured all the machines with the same time zones, even those in different countries. They all shut down to patch at the same time. The entire Bitcoin network stopped following the genesis block and needed to be started again. When they came up, network services and connections were flaky, and the network forked and split, and it was a big mess to say the least. The funny thing is, the code had fewer flaws running on Windows Server than it did on XP.

Those machines are gone now. I replaced them every 12 to 18 months. Servers were donated to several churches and ran email means for such organisations. A couple ran web servers. During the year I started installing machines that ran Windows XP and nodes. There weren't a lot of other machines running Bitcoin in 2009. To my knowledge, Dave ran one machine, that's full-time, and he ran three or four on or off. Hal Finney ran a machine. Bear ran one or two.

I had between 60 and 100 machines running, of which an average of 55 or 56 would be mine personally. In the beginning, 75 were mine personally. There was a lot of supporting infrastructure. The Cisco routers, the switches, the firewalls. I used a combination of IP tables and checkpoint, and had snort running as my IDS.

You might guess, it took up a bit of my time.

The speculation around which Bitcoin belonged to whom always made me laugh. Some of the most clueless pseudoscience ever spouted came out about which Bitcoin Satoshi owned or not.

My old blog, gse-compliance.blogspot.com, was not updated much in this period. You could say, January was a very quiet month. A newly constructed and chucked-together Windows domain is not a fun thing to manage. At the same time, I was still finalising the handover from leaving the accounting firm BDO Kendalls. I was out completely by the third week of January, and it gave me a lot more time than at the start of the month which was hellish.

In 2009, Bitcoin had no established value. So, outside of my personal addresses, I don't know what was actually kept. I doubt that the machines running at the charities or churches I was involved with at the time even exist anymore. My estimate would be that they managed to collect amongst them between 80,000 and 100,000 Bitcoin. If they exist, I hope they do the same people well. You never know, things turn up.

Then, people don't understand the cost associated with running bitcoin. The cost of the Internet connections, the servers, the Microsoft licenses, and the electricity alone came to more than people would care to remember. All up, I spent around AU$1.1 million. As such, between the period of 2007 and mid-2009, I had costs that would be directly attributed to Bitcoin of about 70% of that. I think my mortgage at one stage between the three properties I owned had blown up to around AU$1.4 million.

That was why I needed to sell my ranch.

I said I was owning my past, and in time I'm going to detail all of it. Again, I'm not proud of it all. I've been asked in the past how I managed to get data about criminal networks that I modelled. One of them was because of AnonymousSpeech.com. I used it for email and domain registration, but I also used it personally.

Vistomail was used in what some people would call Canadian pharma spam. Spam didn't originate from the servers, rather the systems that would run globally allowed other people to register domains and fast flux systems that allowed for the control of botnets and compromise of systems around the world. I both helped and hindered some of it.

I helped in that I discussed Bitcoin with people who were associated with a company called High Secured and people who had been using money through Liberty Reserve. Such people were not particularly interested in Bitcoin as money. Liberty Reserve allowed people to take US dollars and transfer them to and from banks without complying with anti-money laundering legislation, so to them Bitcoin wasn't money.

What they did do was use it as a signalling system. Bots were created by people who were associated with something that came from the Russian business network. After the same group of Russian cyber criminals fell apart, some of the parties started their own systems.

Bitcoin enabled them to get past some of the controls that the Microsoft teams had been putting in place. Not because of money, but because a transaction could be used as a signal. If one key signed the transaction, command-and-control servers in a hierarchy would act. If another key was signed, different servers would act. In effect, the systems watched the Bitcoin blockchain and gained instructions without leaving any trace. It helped as a form of covert communication.

Most importantly, for such individuals, Bitcoin started to be a way of controlling the spam servers. I wanted Bitcoin to be used in many ways, and one of them included controlling agents and software instances, but I didn't want where it went. Consequently, I started tracking communications on such networks. Liberty Reserve and High Secured and a few other networks ran my code. I placed back doors in them. At the same time, I ran TCPdump instances and collected traffic. With the machines I had ended up running on such networks, I had a backplane.

The irony is that I both held money on the servers and helped get rid of them.

THE COST OF BITCOIN

Between 2009 and particularly after the end of 2010, the Australian tax office made my life difficult. The two companies I had founded ended up in liquidation as result. I spent over $1 million in legal fees, and with accounting and other losses I think the totals came to around 3 million. The Australian tax office started bankruptcy proceedings during the process. They began in association with the dispute over tax.

The dispute that started here ended in January 2013. The biggest problem started around mid-2011. At that point, I structured my assets. I did so to protect them. The amount of Bitcoin I had at the time was not even something I really cared too much about. It was the intellectual property that mattered; it is what I have fought to protect for the last 20+ years.

In time, I even got to the point where I had the ATO "accept that Dr. Wright did take reasonable care in preparing and lodging his income tax."

Ironically, the tax office then used the liquidation of my companies—which they had caused—to try and have me disbarred as a director. They tried to ban from being a director of any company for a period of 20 years. They lost, but the action also cost me a lot of money.

All my claims baring a small $77 amount were allowed. To offset the $77, I was given an extra $10,000 that I didn't claim but should have. An individual from the Australian tax office even maintained that I should be charged for recklessly under-claiming—but that was quickly thrown out.

All my interest expenses, the travel to and from the farm to manage systems in the claimed amounts of Internet communications for my personal use, were me personally and not my companies, and were allowed.

At this stage, my interest bill alone had come to over $100,000 a year. The loans I had taken out in the previous years all grew. It was eventually allowed and so were the corporate deductions—not that it mattered, because too much had been done to the companies, and they had to go into liquidation.

I get pulled up a lot by people saying that I use people who die to cover up things that have happened. The problem is, I don't know who will die in advance of their death. My grandfather knew Prof David Rees. I attached details of work I had been doing that was based on mathematics and a system called Cocao that Prof. Rees pointed me to many years before. I told the Australian tax office about David Rees in 2009. I was discussing some of his role as I moved assets into other companies again in 2013.

Prof Rees died in August 2013.

At this point, the Australian tax office claimed that I had used Prof. Rees knowing that he would die before they could contact him. Prof. Rees gave me notes on the *Asymptotic Theory of Ideals* (Rees 1988). I use them today. They have been incredibly helpful in some of the work I've been doing. I don't know the future. We are all mortal, and if you need something verified, do it when the person is alive. But the Australian government never really sought to prove anything. They just wanted me gone.

My first marriage ended in October 2010. It had been rocky for a time before it ended. I worked doing forensic contracts only for the prosecution. Some of them didn't involve court. The same side but a completely different aspect of life. October 2010 was when I started to go quiet.

I was offline for much of January 2011. During the time, I had travelled to Venezuela where I was working with a "Jawbreaker" team. The work was focused on stopping the trafficking of humans for the sex trade. I was in "prevention." I did not bring people to justice, I worked with teams to stop things, permanently.

My "Blind Date" in Venezuela had me progressing West to the border of Colombia. It was my last operation of the type. I was shot twice, and evidence of it is likely to still exist on the Internet for all my efforts to have destroyed it. I met with Colombian El Departamento Administrativo de Seguridad (DAS) agents, as my job was accessing systems and information, and on the occasion, it was related to an operation associated with garnishing evidence against FARC-V. Before, I was what some people would call an "agent of influence."

I'm not ashamed of my past, but I never wanted to talk about it. I still do not. The best answer to many aspects of life, the darkened dirty parts, is a solution delivered through a salve of sunshine. So, rather than staying in silence and allowing others to paint a false picture of my life and Bitcoin, I am going to fill in the missing pieces. I always had enough people to be proud of what I did that I did not need to make it public. My uncle knows me well; Don Lynam was very senior within military intelligence, and I grew up respecting him and my grandfather. I saw their sacrifice, and I wanted to emulate some of it.

People smuggling, sex slavery, and many forms of illicit exchange exist in the modern world. People do not like to talk about them. But they exist, and they are insidious, and they are evil that must be stopped.

Terrorist financing occurs because of the existing banking system and the ability to lose transactional data. I worked on Bitcoin for a long time before I found something that would not be able to be used in a manner that was anonymous. A system that economically collapsed to one or none. It needed to be private allowing people to engage in their day-to-day lives and even do things that were mildly wrong. At the same time, it had to be the ultimate anathema to all that was evil in the world.

I designed and created Bitcoin to stop the need for people like me—people who worked with SAD operatives and even those acting in the tracing of funds.

I was a pastor for a time. But, the images of what I have done, what I have seen, and the cruelties I have witnessed in the world led me to abandon the position. I have witnessed children as young as 10 with AK-47s and women who have been forced to watch the death of their children knowing that other members of their family are being held and, if they try to escape, will be killed. All of it exists because of a system that allows records to be lost.

I designed Bitcoin to create an immutable evidence trail, money that is private and yet does not suffer the fate of Gyges. Anonymity is a curse. Nothing good comes of it.

I came back from Colombia and Venezuela already rather disillusioned. The first thing I found was Bitcoin being used in the dark web. I discovered the creation I had given birth to—something I designed to bring light—was being used for all the worst reasons. Not only drugs, but people. Silk Road didn't blatantly advertise people the way that they did drugs and guns, there are other names for everything, yet people know what is being exchanged.

And I saw my creation twisted into something I despised, and I entered a deep abyss of despair. Eventually, later in 2011, I started working on the solution to the problem I had birthed. The start of the company called Panopticrypt. Since then, I have worked on a number of creations that connect alongside Bitcoin and in fact any consensus system. Silk Road did not create a world without force. It allowed people not only to sell drugs and to engage in the low-end overly hyped media-fuelled dark-web store that enabled people to sell credit-card information, commit fraud, and even sell people.

Children between the age of 12 and 16 were exchanged using Silk Road. Some were forced into prostitution, and others were sold to work as beggars in the US and Western European streets. In the years that Silk Road operated, over 1,000 children were exchanged in Western Europe through the north-eastern Italian corridor— bought and sold using terms that allowed so on Silk Road and bypassing the filters, so they maintained plausible deniability.

Some of the children were kidnapped, and others promised a better life. Terre des Hommes (https://www.tdh.ch/en) is a good source if you want to learn about the impact of such an illicit trade.

Such is your hero if you worship and praise to the idol of *Free Ross*. It is a story that is told of free trade and friendly people engaging in commerce without the nasty state intervening. They neglected an essential part of the story. They forgot the people who were trafficked. They forget the lives of those damaged forever because of hard drugs. They ignore the dealers who use it to fool other people into a lie and allow them to be captured into a web of deceit.

Bitcoin started to seem to me to be delivering everything I was opposed to, and everything I thought it was designed not to be started to appear. So, all I can say is that I was disillusioned.

Even Hal started to get it. In December 2010, Hal said:

> *Ultimately, it's good for the network for mining to be expensive. It makes it that much harder for a well-financed attacker to dominate the network.*

So, unlike the earlier idea of needing to put a cap on and slowly build to allow many nodes, he started to get it. Unfortunately, by that time I was already disillusioned.

He still saw Bitcoin as the store-of-value and digital-gold ideal, though.

> *I see Bitcoin as ultimately becoming a reserve currency for banks, playing much the same role as gold did in the early days of banking. Banks could issue digital cash with greater anonymity and lighter weight, more efficient transactions.*

He never got around to understanding how efficient Bitcoin can be. I guess we all have baggage that weighs us down from the ideas we had before. For Hal, it was the cypherpunk concept of money and digital cash. It is not what Bitcoin is, nor what it was designed to be.

What I have learned, and I have learned the lesson very well, is that you cannot teach other people and you cannot make them learn. You can provide material and give them a path to learning.

With people like Hal, I've come to learn that no matter how much you like someone, it is not worth investing in saving one person from a flawed idea to the exclusion of offering a means of teaching others. I have learned the hard way not to focus on an individual, not to try and save them but rather to get material out allowing as many people as possible to learn — and first those who seek to learn.

Learning is a privilege, not a right. It must be earnt. It is a proof of work. Some people think that it's important for me to come out and bring everybody in as quickly as I can.

My time, as with everyone's, is incredibly limited. We live short fast lives, and unlike many people, I do not have time to waste. So, I only want the people who really want to learn. The people who are going to take what they have learnt and create and build and grow the ecosystem.

I didn't run away from Bitcoin, but I needed to know more about the system I created. Most critically, I needed to know that it could work at scale as I had planned. Towards the end of 2010, WikiLeaks had started promoting Bitcoin as an end to their woes. WikiLeaks and I have not had a good relationship.

I was angry at this. I was angry with Dave Kleiman when he didn't tell me how badly off he was. I was angry with people taking a system I created and changing it to something else.

Everybody looks at Bitcoin now, and thinks it's worth so much, so I must have always known I'd be rich.

I didn't.

I saw myself as a failure in 2011. Bitcoin was a long way from being finished.

The funny thing is, the people later proved I was right. Because of Bitcoin, Silk Road was stopped, and many of the people behind it are now in prison. It didn't make things easier at the time, but it is a nice vindication now.

I needed to go away, and I needed to prove to myself that the system I had created worked the way I'd intended. It does, and it always did.

Such is some of the irony I see in attempts to create something that Bitcoin was designed not to be, to try and make it more into something that Hal and Wei would've designed.

I started the company Panopticrypt in June 2011.

At this stage, I was still deep in disputes with the Australian tax office. My two companies that I'd formed in 2009, Information Defense and Integers, were beyond saving. As with everything in my past, it was the intellectual property I fought to keep, not the money. Nothing has changed now. Even the battles in the early days of nChain were about keeping control of the direction and vision I seek. Unfortunately, we even had a few people wanting to research Ethereum and other coins and other consensus mechanisms. I handle such things better now than I did.

I have not trusted many people in my life.

Doing so has lost me many friends over the years. In part, it has come from my expectations and in other parts a conflict between what we seek. Dave Kleiman was a friend for a long time and perhaps one of the very few people I think I could ever keep trusting.

I have friendships that failed and that I regret not having maintained. My intellectual property, the systems I create are the things that hold the highest value in my life and have done so throughout my life. I've sacrificed and thrown away many things on the altar of potential creation.

Peter Robinson worked for me in Sydney. It was for one of the early iterations of a company I had called DeMorgan. It's perhaps been nearly 20 years and certainly over 15 since I spoke last with Peter.

Peter was a good guy, he is a damn good coder even if he hadn't gone to university, and when he put his mind to something, he could achieve a lot. Unfortunately, his goals were different to mine, and he was working for me. He had a software application that he wanted to develop. Some small parts of it helped in what I was doing in the early days, before I knew what I was doing, but it was never something that particularly interested me. Unfortunately, it was something that Peter wanted to do. Here's the trouble; if you have a friend who works for you, you have choices to make. Do you put the business first or your friendship?

If you want your business to be successful, your friendship has to take a backseat.

I also started a company called Strasan in 2011 with other people who were friends at the time. Unfortunately, the other people in the company wanted something different than I wanted. I'm willing to look for the long term. To take a risk at creating something great. I know the story of Achilles, and I choose a path that few would. Achilles could've faded, he could've had a life without sorrow and without pain, and yet he chose one that would immortalise his name and what he achieved. Right now, you haven't seen what is coming, and people think that Bitcoin and blockchain is the big invention, but it's just a Lego block. It's a Lego block that was needed in the creation and that if not available, if not solved, and if not incentive-based would not have led to solutions that will create the Metanet.

After two years of earning very little but spending a lot on my research, I saw what I created as it started to become the thing I despised.

Dave was already ill in 2011, and I pushed him further. The only way I could fund and further the research that I had been doing to stop that which I saw developing was derived from gambling. Dave oversaw the operations. There are other people who are still around and that are associated with the Costa Rica operation, but I will never name them. We used Liberty Reserve to hold funds and pay people.

It is ironic that the only way I saw to fix the problem that I created was to utilise something even worse. In early 2013, the US government seized funds and stopped the operations of Liberty

Reserve. The money I was using to pay for computers and operations stopped.

Bitcoin didn't fail, but other parts of my life did. I used to own horses. When I sold my property, I had to sell them too. A horse I had owned for a decade, a mean grumpy thing like me. I had to give him away. It broke my heart.

Say what you want, that it was only an animal, but I interacted with them more than I did with many people. Outside of Dave and my property, I had a very isolated life. At one point, I was doing four post-graduate degrees simultaneously, and I was working. The period includes my master's degree in law and a master's degree in statistics. I needed such information to complete Bitcoin, but at the same time, it left me isolated. I had work, my farm, and one really good friend—Dave.

Dave started getting sick in 2011, and I knew that I had to give up my farm.

I did isolated forensic jobs, and did work for a number of casinos and sports betting sites such as Centerbet to try and keep some money coming in, but the first thing I needed to do was actually prove that Bitcoin worked.

It was the nature of what I did with Panopticrypt between 2011 and 2013. Nothing that I could commercialise and make money out of, just rule research so I would know that I hadn't wasted my life completely.

I spent millions testing alternatives. I needed to be certain I was correct. That the system worked as a commercial solution and that something like a home-user version was not valid. Or, at least that if it was, it would not end as a crime coin. I worked to create a mainstream system and making an anonymous coin would have simply ended me.

I worked out how systems such as Monero, Zcash, and for that matter any anonymous blockchain could be infiltrated and stopped.

I needed to work with many organizations and some quite unsavoury characters to do so. I'm not talking about the honest licensed gaming companies and other types that used Liberty Reserve. This was a part of the problem. Dave had been storing all the money we used in accounts attached to Liberty Reserve. It's not as much of a problem for me as it was for him because gambling laws in the US preclude sports betting in any form whereas it is legal in Australia.

Dave and I worked with law enforcement and others for a long time. Dave took opiates, because his condition left him in constant pain. But more importantly, contacts of his told him about the impending takedown of Liberty Reserve eight weeks before it occurred. He was left with the problem of knowing that if he moved his funds, it would be tracked. Effectively, to do so would have ended his career.

Rock, hard place.

Frying pan, fire.

If David had talked to me about his problems with money, I would have helped. When it comes to work, I'm rather excessive and focused. My wife will tell you I hyper focus, the world moves around me, and I do what needs to be done. It is how we have gotten to completing over a thousand white papers and how I had 20 academic papers accepted for publication in the last two months. I can't say it's good, it takes a toll in anyone's life, but you could say I'm driven.

Where we are with the Metanet now has come about following another decade of research. I did not have a clue about how to do it until last year. What you've seen is the equivalent of the Internet circa 1991. We have a lot more coming; it is just not public quite yet. What people are seeing as development in BSV is nothing compared to what is about be released.

I wanted to bring my inventions back into Australia, but I also needed to do so without shooting myself in the head. I wanted to remain as secret as I could and repatriate funds to Australia. I was still doing a lot of contract work with government, and even acted as a prosecution expert, and conducted judge prosecutor training.

I always believed that if Bitcoin would eventually scale enough for my ideas to have a chance to succeed, nothing could stop it. I was also afraid that it wouldn't make it to the stage it needed to reach to continue to grow. If I had been able to at the time, I would have patented everything to do with Bitcoin. Unfortunately, there was no way possible that I could see that would have allowed me to do so. Satoshi, the issuer of a monetary system, can be close to anonymous, though even then I wasn't. But you cannot file an intellectual-property claim using a pseudonym.

More importantly, filing patents globally is incredibly expensive. My guess is that each patent is costing us between $25K and $70K, and right now we are approaching a total of 700 that have been processed. You can do the maths.

In life, as in Bitcoin, it is hard to remain anonymous. I ended up with quite a few people finding things and trying to blackmail me and threaten me over the years.

I just thought it would work out, because it's there, and right.

Unfortunately, it doesn't always work that way. The reality is, there are always people who don't like what you're doing.

The core developers, of course, propagated this idea that Bitcoin is not private enough. None of them understand that there have been many, many forms of anonymous money. It's very simple. You have an app. You have a wallet. and the police go, "We're taking it."

People say, "You can't do that."

Fact is, you can. The mere possession of the thing becomes illegal.

I moved to the UK in October 2015. We still had business interests there, so I would fly to and from Australia, but my home was already in Wimbledon, London.

In 2016, I was dressed in a turtleneck. The PR people had the idea that they would transform me into the vision of a genius that the world wants to see. The idea was a poor copy of Steve Jobs. The flaw here comes from looking backwards. When he started, Jobs was the outsider. He was rejected and fought to grow what he was building every day. The attempted building of an alternative version of what I created goes against all I stand for. Yet, I allowed myself to get into such a position.

I should say, I allowed myself to be dressed as the image that another saw as marketable, and I did not have the courage to stop and say no. Or I did, but at (close to) the worst possible time.

I like to wear suits. I enjoy wearing ties. So is my choice, and with wealth comes the right to decide. In my case, I plan to dress as the nerd in a three-piece suit. I like how I dress, and I am comfortable. I do not make my team wear suits nor dress as I do, I choose it for myself. I am comfortable in a suit.

I had a lot of friends, many in the police and military, who I have abandoned. I am going to come out of the dark and start finding them again, and I hope that they all understand my lost decade.

I was embittered for many years.

Creation is mostly long hours of boring and repetitive work. It is not about making a fast buck, and it is all that ICOs are not. Bitcoin was created to be a means to allow the world both to commoditise information and to create sound money.

Bitcoin is the balancing point between what is just able to be totally legal and stop crime and what is acceptable. It's the neutral knife point. It can't be a state tool for oppression. It can't be an anarchist thing. It has to be right down the middle. Nevada. Neutral. We don't care.

I was not afraid of Gavin when he met with the CIA. Bitcoin is an immutable data store, that is something that honest government desires. I was saddened and disillusioned by Silk Road and the dark web. I needed to complete what I called "other things," and I have done so now.

Silk Road failed because of Bitcoin's design. No blockchain will ever be crime friendly. Such is the nature of the system. The audit trail allows the authorities to track from one criminal to another. We saw it in action as Silk Road was taken down, then Silk Road 2.0 was taken down, and then the corrupt FBI agent who stole Bitcoin was caught and arrested. Bitcoin is sunshine. It is the cure for the festering wound that is corruption, be that from government or from criminal groups.

Many people will be desperate to discredit me, no matter what I say or do. The thing is, the more they now seek to discredit me, the more I am going to release. When I finish, even Atlas will shrug.

They don't want me to be Satoshi. They don't want a guy who is ex-military, who worked with the prosecution side of the law, who worked with the government to protect law to be Satoshi. They want to have the equivalent of eCash. They want it to be anonymous. They want it to be anti-everything. Down with the state.

They don't want to admit their own failures. That's part of it. And a lot of people, that's how they look at things. If I come along, then their excuse to say, "Well, I can't do this," disappears.

I am in uni all the time, and I'm working, and I've got a family. They don't want to know that. They don't want someone who works hard and studies. They want a myth. The smart genius who walks in and does everything, because then is no threat to their ego. They want to be able to say, "This guy is super smart because he's a young guy who's reinvented all this stuff."

And then, if you have someone like me, you have to say, "He worked hard. That means if I want to do this, I have to work hard. If I want to make an excuse, it's because I didn't work hard." Richard Feynman said it well. He said, "I'm not smarter than everyone. I just work harder." And he went and got himself a Nobel prize and a whole lot of other physics prizes and discovered a lot of tensor mathematics and physics and quantum stuff that most people wouldn't even have a clue what it means.

Bitcoin is a story of myths; it was never designed for such an end, but it's what it has become. To some, it is easier; the myth to them becomes stronger than reality.

I had a lot of help along the way. Without Hal, the code would have crashed time after time. I am not going to list the people who helped me here, but Bitcoin started because of my ideas. It was my design, and it is my creation.

Making certain that it cannot be subverted by criminals is and remains my duty.

People in the group of companies and others pushed for me to come out in 2016 to clear up the lies. I was afraid. If I start to tell the truth of Bitcoin, it is to also open my past. It means that I am going to open all the dark secrets, and when I do, many more will follow. I spent over 25 years working in places many would not believe exist in a modern world, and once Pandora opens the box, there is no way to stop the secrets coming out. It was my lack of courage — the fear of what can come from my past and the need for courage to face the future that stopped me before.

I am opening the box.

Please do not think it is the end of the story. It is only starting. Bitcoin changes the world, and I have enough courage to follow through now.

Jimmy Nguyen, BSV CEO, has said not to comment on it, but I will. To be open is to be open. Bitcoin has an issuer. It is a system that is set in stone and when changed is a new system with an airdrop, so a fork is a new system. I am the issuer for Bitcoin. There is no decentralised here. The only protection I had was remaining unknown. As I prove who I am, I prove who the issuer is for Bitcoin. The issuer of a money system who did not ask for permission and knows that it was not legal when it occurred. Bitcoin (BSV) was issued in 2009. BTC was issued with an airdrop in 2017.

I don't think people understand what it's like to sacrifice nearly everything you have for decades to try and create something. Worse, to be left in a position where you think it has failed. Some of what drove me was the anger from all these events, but at the same time the mere act of creation is a reward and a drug.

Like it or not, I'm not going away. In all of it, through all the pain I managed to prove and solve and find the way forward.

Truth is not derived from a code-is-law perspective. You cannot sign truth with the digital key. Some want to do so, but it's because they hate law. I don't. I did when I was young. Some of my outlooks were similar to those we see in Core Coin (BTC) now, but over time, I have changed and learned that law is important, and so is process. So, like it or not, I'm going to do it my way.

You see, I have a long-term outcome and a long-term outlook. And sometimes you will discover that it is better to allow people to go on and have them think that you're less of a threat because of what you do. When you think it through, if you think it through, you may start to understand.

I have mentioned adopting a persona. I posted the strategy publicly in 2017.

> *Feign madness but keep your balance. 假痴不癫／假痴不癫 Hide behind the mask of a fool, a drunk, or a madman to create confusion about your intentions and motivations. Lure your opponent into underestimating your ability until, overconfident, he drops his guard. Then you may attack.*

I left people believing that I was doing one thing based on the Twitter persona, which they addressed as if it was a reality they should take note of. At the same time, I filed multiple papers and have presented at several academic conferences. My two PhDs that I'm currently doing, in law at the University of Leicester and applied mathematics at CNAM, are going well. At the same time, we have filed just under 800 patent applications. There are at least 1280 white papers in the pipeline that will lead to patents.

Simultaneously, the team has managed to obtain a sustained transaction rate of around 1,000 transactions per second. By the end of the year, we will be able to handle a transaction volume the level of Visa.

Meanwhile, many of the people who want to discredit me attack me personally. This is a common form of attack when the attacker can't fault the logic of an argument, and so turns their attention to the proponent of the argument, rather than the argument itself.

We see this in law, where a lawyer unable to fault the evidence instead seeks to discredit the witness, in politics where spin doctors seek to dig up dirt on political opponents to detract from unpopular policy decisions, and in the media. It's called the genetic fallacy and is also known as the fallacy of origins, or the fallacy of virtue.

The genetic fallacy avoids an argument by shifting the focus onto something's or someone's origins. It's similar to an ad hominem fallacy in the sense that it leverages existing negative perceptions to make someone's argument look bad, without actually presenting a case for why the argument itself lacks merit.

The origin of the claim is presented as a basis for why the claim is true or false.

In one specific case, it comes down to arguments about the people. Bitcoin is technology. You know the other side of the argument is failing when it has moved to attacking a person rather than the argument itself.

It is a common tactic in the world of social media. Proof of social media is not about truth but rather about a deception that can change and mutate over time. It is one of the aspects of Bitcoin that have been developed that allows for a system of truth. If you view my videos and presentations from 2014, you will see that I have the same outlook and concept of Bitcoin now as I had then.

When evaluating an argument, it is better to go to the source and not to take modified versions of information. Biased media sources colour articles in a manner designed to prepare a response from the reader or listener. In part, it is why the post-modern "thinker" is one who follows them without thinking, askew science and the modern legal process.

Like it or not, Bitcoin and other cryptocurrencies do not stop you from paying tax. They are not designed for such a purpose. Rather, they can facilitate fair taxation. It is possible to integrate a value-added tax directly into Bitcoin using script. Doing so would allow an organisation to pay its VAT instantly on the sale of goods or services. Further, it can be integrated in such a way that even a reversal from the customer would allow instant and automated taxes to still apply without fraud.

Nor do I seek to save people. If you're a speculator, if you're invested in that fake copy of Bitcoin, BTC, then I don't care, it's your problem. I have something to build, and I figure it's a 20- to 30-year journey to get it created properly. Oh, in the next four or five years, you'll start to see just how big it is, but it's nothing compared to where it's going in the decades to come.

I didn't go to what was at one stage millions in debt to own Bitcoin. I went into debt, I worked hard and long and smart, and studied, and gave up most of what people need and seek and want and love and enjoy for the chance to create something.

Like it or not, I am Satoshi.

FREEDOM OF SPEECH VERSUS PRIVACY

Many of those arguing for anonymity are truly arguing only for their own privacy, while they argue for free speech to gain power and control over others. If we consider the criminal violation by certain individuals of controls designed to provide privacy, we start to see the hypocrisy in the argument.

In the European Union, there is an implied right to privacy. It is a fundamental human right. The right to free speech allows you to stand in a public place and talk if people will listen. It is not a right to fence them in and make them listen, nor is it a right for an audience. It is not a right to come to someone else's talk and talk them down or talk over them, nor is it a right to be heard. Those who try to force an audience to listen say that they are fighting for freedom, and yet they are crushing the privacy rights of others.

Privacy means that you can exclude people. If we cannot have private spaces where we can exclude other people, then we have nothing. Everyone needs some space where information can be shared with others in private, to discuss secrets, plan, and even set a rate on information. The rate on free speech and privacy allows us to charge people for coming and listening to us and to exclude those who won't pay the rate. And it is not monetary in all cases. It can be as simple as being polite.

Knowledge asymmetry is important. We own the rights to all our labour. The current socialism of the mind is a pernicious attack on the rights of man. The attack against intellectual property is an attack against the right of labour. All labour starts within and through the human mind. If an ox or horse works in a field, it will gain nothing. It is the human controlling it who gains the benefit of his and their work, and likewise, it is the human mind which creates all value.

In bypassing privacy controls, those who create bots and other systems to breach controls over computer systems radically alter how people interact.

Social media has become the cesspit it is because of the creative commons. People expect everything for free. The result is that trolls operate at the same level as the erudite. That those who want to interact to gain knowledge can be drowned out in the sea of ignorance that surrounds those who are paid to attack. It is what Bitcoin cures. Such individuals who act as trolls are Sybils. They are parties without value.

Information comes at a cost.

Not all costs are monetary, some are societal, and the way we act in the way we interact is a cost. Trolls bypass the ability to form rational relationships. They take away the ability to act in a manner that is civil and polite. In particular, they force us into a position of acting as an aggrieved party. You do not have an unlimited right to free speech in all contexts. Even the U.S. Constitution does not allow you to walk into another person's home and tell him or her your feelings. You do not have the right to invade the privacy of another and force your views on him or her. It is an attack on free speech.

The ability to block trolls on social media is critical. The ability to stop people, to make them act within societal bounds is critical.

In 2015, I was forced into a position that ultimately put every aspect of my life under a microscope. Contrary to popular opinion, at no point did I agree to sign publicly on a web page. One thing I've learnt in the interceding years is the ignorance of people and the inability of them to read past the headline.

The ability to exclude others has value. You must act within the bounds of society if you want to be able to talk and interact without being excluded. It is not a bad thing; it is how culture and society develop. It is how children grow up and stop being toddlers throwing tantrums.

And yet, it is what many seek; they want chaos and a world they can watch burn.

A part of free speech is learning and understanding the art of rhetoric and how you interact with others. I have had many faces and worn many masks. Others get to maintain privacy, whether you create something does not change the right to it. So, people's need to understand my life is not their right.

Well, I get the guilty pleasure of watching those who seek to attack me end in pain. It is not something I'm proud of, but then, I'm human.

As a result of many things that I have not wanted, I'm going to have to go into court and verify properly my involvement with Bitcoin. I'm particularly not looking forward to doing so. It's going to result in a lot of people losing money very quickly.

Some would always lose. There's nothing I can do about it, but I did hope to minimise the losses and bring it down simply and easily. But like it or not, I am going to be in court this year, and like it or not, I don't have the choice. I did all I could to hide and suppress information concerning the development of Bitcoin and much more, but in the next 12 to 18 months, there will not be much left in secret about the start of the system. In a way, it saddens me.

Trust me, it won't stop me.

I will simply do my utmost to suppress as much as I can. Some things will remain with the court and only be revealed within the privacy of the court. The problem, of course, is that there are no steganographic controls that one can place across talking. Even when there is a court order protecting privacy, we already know that such things leak. I'm not holding it against the court or law. Even with orders stopping the dissemination of information, people talk. So is reality, and I understand.

It saddens me, because it was my right to privacy and not your right to know.

I did all I could to muddy the waters. I did all I could to stay private and have a life with parts that remain mine. Early on, I could even put up with the false claims of fraud, knowing that in the long term it's not going to matter, but people are going to discover that they have made an error that they are going to be very sorry for.

I spent a long time designing Bitcoin, there are few flaws left. The code needs work still, but it is a separate thing to the protocol. People fail to understand that decentralisation is about power. The only way to decentralise power is to affix and set the protocol immutably and allow no change. A system that can be altered is not decentralised.

I did not really want to act; I wanted to sit and design and allow others to build, but it seems I do not get such a privilege, I do not get to be the architect, but need to take responsibility for my creations.

Unfortunately for many, it is going to be painful. Bitcoin is a protocol and platform, and it is designed in such a way that in the end, only one will survive. We don't publish patents until we need to. We are not a normal Silicon Valley company that needs to seek money but rather one that can stay in the shadows and push and steer the direction of the world. Soon, you are going to see what it all means.

But then, many of you have taken my rights. You forced me to act when I did not want to, and you are about to see what it means. We will start with one or two and move from there and doing so will lead to the collapse of the whole Ponzi as the dominoes fall one after another.

As you discover what I am and what I have, you are going to discover that I plan and plot over the decades.

It is a human right to privacy; not allowing but having others force their way into your home, onto your property, that is acting outside the bounds that are set on them, means to allow chaos and restrict freedom.

It is an attack on the rights of humanity to force others to listen to what you have to say. You have no right to make other people hear you. Allowing criminal and illegal systems and people who commit hate crime is not free speech, nor is it part of what a company can legally allow. It is an attack on society.

Lucky for me, I have the resources at hand and the help of others that allow me to weather it and more, to cause more damage to my enemies in their attack on freedom than they can imagine. What you did not want is about to happen. When we go to court, you will see how much pain will result on your end and how little comes to mine.

I did not want to have to go down such a path, I did not want to give up my privacy, but please understand; though I have a long timeframe, I also remember and act.

Any blockchain can be controlled and made to work within the legal frameworks of where it exists. It does not stop government taxing, and it does not bring down banks. It was never designed for such a purpose.

A blockchain is a system that is incredibly private when the people using it remain within the limits of the law. It is conversely incredibly simple to trace when the parties to a transaction have breached the law, and it allows a complete audit trail to exist. The past is something people do not understand, and few have learnt. In the 90s, a far more anonymous electronic cash system was developed, and since then, many others have been created.

Bitcoin solves the issue as it has no single party which can fail and, with such collapse, take down the entire system. It was never about all users running nodes, and it is certainly not about equality or taking down the establishment.

THE BURDEN OF PROOF

In 2016, I could have come forward and jumped through many hoops in a vain attempt to have people "like and accept me." It is not a result that will ever be achieved. The "crypto" community is not seeking Satoshi. They want a constructed myth that allows them to believe they can have an anonymous system of money and that those things parliaments seek to stop, they can allow.

They would not want me, as the system I created is not anonymous and it cannot be made to be anonymous. The nature of a "blockchain" is a system that acts as an immutable and admissible evidence stop that binds both the individual and the system they exist within.

In 2016, I wasn't ready. I hadn't planned on being outed in 2015. But the "sign publicly, and everyone will know" mantra doesn't prove anything, and the people doing the calling know that perfectly well. Of course, what they are also selling is a quick fix. None of them want Bitcoin. They're all seeking something different and trying to change the system to deliver it. In vain. Because that way, they would get rich in a Ponzi scheme, and say they tried their best when the house of cards comes inevitably crashing down.

In May 2016, I concluded that the best I could hope for in signing publicly and doing everything that would be needed would be the exact opposite of proof. I would start by signing; and then there would be other questions. Greedy and undeserving individuals would come out expecting much more and saying that somehow, I had stolen keys that I never had access to (it does not matter that it is not actually possible let alone feasible on Bitcoin). It would no longer be enough to try and blackmail me into making them instantly rich, but to see a long-term gravy train.

Most people, even those in "crypto," don't understand Bitcoin. There are those I trust and those I don't. They fail to understand that you cannot simply steal someone's keys without access. They fail to see the issues that collapsed eCash, and they rarely care. But such is the problem; Bitcoin is a completely new narrative. It alters everything, and in 20 to 30 years from now, people will not recognise the world we are in because of Bitcoin.

A DECADE AGO

When I started mining Bitcoin, it was important that many machines ran.

Remember, it was before Bitcoin had a price. What you will find is that the IP addresses and locations of the machines don't match. If you start analysing how early versions of Bitcoin operate and how they operate on different platforms, you'll start to understand the difference.

- How does Windows XP SP2 vs SP3 operate?
- How does Vista operate?
- How does a grouping of machines differ when put on a single network class?
- Has any testing been done of any such theories?
- Does domain versus workgroup make a difference?
- How about Windows time services?

All of these are valid scientific questions. None of them have been answered, nor have they even been asked. Such ignorance forms the false narrative that surrounds Bitcoin. Again, Vistomail utilised credit card payments in 2008.

Interestingly, nobody thinks to check simple facts like that. They want a story told by cypherpunks of a myth that cannot exist and a lie of Utopia they dream will bring equality and communist unity. The fact of the matter is: evidence is simple. They just don't want you to see it. It doesn't suit their false narrative.

Instead, they call for me to sign using the early keys.

There is a real problem with such a call. There are several downsides I will not discuss and a couple I will. You ask to see my keys; well, you are in effect asking to see my bank statement. That is the opposite of what Bitcoin is about. I really do not care if you like that you cannot tell what I have or do not have. It is a form of information asymmetry that I desire to preserve.

The likes of Bill Gates and Mark Zuckerberg have a large amount of non-liquid wealth. It is known. What they do not disclose is how much wealth they can deploy.

Most critically, why should I? What am I to gain in return? You see, it is a contract negotiation, and you have little or nothing I desire. Sorry, but so is the entirety of the scenario. Informational asymmetry allows me to have some level of consideration that I can exchange. What are you offering for it?

Gavin knows I have the early keys. What does it matter?

If I choose to sign for some and not others, it is my choice. I could, but it would require something I value in return, and it is not money.

If I sign, the next attack is simple: I stole the keys. No matter what I do, there is no path from PoSM (proof of social media) to acceptance for me. More, it does not matter. All that does is what is created.

Will I create more, if I parade as a monkey before the grinder on the stage and dance? No. I would lose the time and ability to create.

I would be dancing on the string that fame requires. So again, I reject such a path. Building is the only truth path. Creation.

There is a lot of money being made in the false narrative that Bitcoin and associated systems are there to free the world for anarchy. More importantly, there are a lot of people making money in insider trading and pumping vacuous penny-share offers in a manner that has been done every decade as people tend so easily to forget the last scam. None of them want what Bitcoin is. To them, Bitcoin is the antichrist, the bringer of the end, and all they desire not to be. For Bitcoin leaves an unalterable trail of all the scammers and all the false information.

It is the Enrons, the Maddoffs and the Charles Ponzis that seek for records to be forever lost.

No matter what I do, I will never live up to the standards that some people want. The reason is, I am not what people want. I am not an anarchist, I do not believe in a world without government, and I do not have thoughts of a world without banking.

Bitcoin does not bring capital funding to the unbanked in and of itself. It is a depository and a form of money that allows for payment and very simple saving but does not introduce capital raising and many of the other aspects that banks provide. Bitcoin can be the foundation of a system that allows the unbanked to become banked. It does not start with anonymity; it requires identity and reputation.

People don't seem to understand that I don't do the accounts or filings or other things for myself. I use companies, individuals, employees, and more. My companies used company secretarial services. Like it or not, you'll start to find that it is not me behind the company shares, issues, or updates. It's not me when it comes to the filing either.

I am completely and utterly horrible at such things. That's why I leave them to other people. Then again, some of them have been worse than me.

I do not even manage my LinkedIn profile. To tell the truth, I haven't even looked at it.

The stupidity of some of the soon-to-be-debunked claims about me is that the people making them don't care about truth. They seek anything to discredit me. Some of the accusations come from their lack of understanding how things work within organisations. They see themselves acting on their own accounts or finances or sending something to the tax man and think that's how everyone else's life happens to be.

Mine isn't.

When there are errors in files, it isn't because of some malicious construction, but rather errors happen in files and filing. My current EA is brilliant. She does a great job. I've had people in the past who though very nice have not been incredibly efficient. The funny thing is, we have documents that are being compiled wrong and it is easy to determine as being an error. Yet people do not want to look and see the discrepancies that are clear but seek to find something to discredit me. Doing so is what protects their false idea of what Bitcoin is about.

One of the biggest problems people harp on is that of contracts that have been filed in error. There is one document on the Internet right now that is a compilation of separate documents that are not related. Unfortunately, when they were put together, they were saved in the same file.

On one page of the document, it calls for *appendix a*. Following it is *appendix 1*. In one section, it calls for a schedule, and then there is an appendix. The fonts change. There is a cover document, and if you actually look at the full document, there are nine pages in total in the purported seven-page document. Yet nobody thought to check whether it was a single document before jumping on it and saying it proves me wrong.

So, going forward is going to be fun. We now have more patents in play than any of the large global players, and going forward, my intellectual property, not just Bitcoin but all of it, is going to determine the path taken by many aspects of the world for years to come.

PROOF ENDS WORK

There are those I trust and those I don't. I trust some of my business partners such as Jimmy, Calvin, and others I will not name, but some people would prefer a quick win. They just want to make money and get out. I saw it all too clearly in 2016. More importantly, others that I am not involved with would use it in a manner that I could never accept.

As soon as I conclusively give everything I know, it will be used for a quick pump followed by a very quick dump. Not one part of it will lead to Bitcoin being implemented or innovators building.

Such was the dilemma I had to face in 2016 and then even in 2017, when I started to appear again. What happens, if too many people simply believe not because of work but mere belief? Uninformed religious dogma has filled the space. It is going to take a long time to slowly teach people how Bitcoin works and what it delivers.

I can't do so unless I work. I understand that the path which I've chosen is something that will sit on my shoulders for a long time. It is not one where people adore me or like what I'm saying but rather one of truth. It is the harder path and the longer path.

My part is to build and teach. There are people who I will choose to categorically prove to. And those people are ones that will also have a hard path, for we will be building.

The biggest difficulty is not simply aligning people or finding something that can align long-term. My vision, path, and strategy will take many years. Not the 10 that have been seen publicly with Bitcoin nor the 10 before that, but decades more from here and the point we're at. In doing so, there are certain things I can do very well and others that are best handed off to others.

The dilemma, simply put, stems from trust. In Bitcoin, trust comes through an investment. Miners must put large amounts of capital into a competitive system that works if they support the system. Long-term, the miners who do not support the growth of the system will find themselves in a severely depleted capital scenario. In Bitcoin, we have a signalling method that allows people to easily understand the investment and support within the system. The difficulty comes when considering one's own life.

In my case, there isn't a simple external proof-of-work derivative that I can use. Others can see it from me. I've completed over 1,200 white papers that will result in a total of 2 to 3 patents for each white paper. We are scaling Bitcoin, and later in the year, we will have more transactional capacity than Visa and MasterCard combined.

With everything in life, we need to choose what we do and how we focus. In my case, my involvement in the accounting, day-to-day management, and financial aspects of the company are minimal. The times that I have focused on such areas I do not excel at resulted in the consequences of not being able to produce the best results in what matters most, research and development. Consequently, you either focus where you are best or fail.

The difficulty comes in signalling from others. In early 2016, I didn't trust my own instincts, and I was a led down a path that I did not like. I understand why people did so. There are always the ones who want a quick return. I understand it perfectly well; for a small investment, a small part of something, why not take the opportunity to make a multi-billion-dollar sale where your investment will increase 10 times or more in a matter of months? I get it perfectly well, and so is the problem.

Can I definitively prove who I am? Yes. I can. But, what does it achieve long term? Doing things too quickly leads to trouble.

It's not a matter of signing with keys alone. There are people who already know I could do so and which of the early keys they saw, and know I have access to, yet it does nothing to help with repudiation.

There is a problem in the cryptographic community in thinking that code creates law. Or, for that matter, that code can capture the real world. It doesn't and it can't. There is no such thing as non-repudiation. A few academics residing in ivory towers like to believe cryptographic solutions can be achieved here, and many fools believe them. Unfortunately, such people ignore law. The key is not identity. It can be shared, stolen, copied, or assigned. In a court, you must attest to a key. So, the funny thing is, all the people such as Wired asking "How do I prove?" and going to the people who don't want proof is so much of a joke.

My issue is something that many in the past would understand. When Getty had to consider what would happen after he finished, for the fate of his company, the issue was succession. He worked to the very end as shall I. But what about other people?

My goal is creation. It is building something that will last. It's not about being nice or liked, it is simply creating a structure that's going to last. One that will not have people selling out under me and one that allows people to build over time. I understand the temptation very well. Money is incredibly addictive. Maintaining the balance is something that takes a lot of discipline and work in ensuring that you don't give up the reason you have wealth.

There is also power in keeping something to yourself. There is a little vestige in that you can make sure people will hold on and keep building and not take the easy gain and stop. I don't want to be remembered because I was yet another billionaire or I came up with an idea and moved on. I seek nothing less than creating a commercial replacement for the entire Internet. One that solves the tragedy of the commons and at the same time provides a global commodity that becomes a money. A sound money. A global money and the means of measuring economic information as we move into an information economy.

I would like to have far more publications, and I am working on it.

But mostly, I intend to see Bitcoin scale into a global economic system and become the plumbing for the information world.

So, I'm not asking for you to believe me. I really don't care. I have set up an evidential trail that now insures my place in history. Something people don't understand about Bitcoin is that it is also a time lock. Bitcoin with nLockTime allows for the pseudonymous release of information at defined times. It's a concept that I took from Asimov. It is aimed to ensure that information is provably released when the author chooses. Only when the author chooses.

So, no matter what happens to me, I know my place in history.

It's a very good feeling that one. I will also say that I am far from done. It's taken me 20 years to build the foundation, and now the edifice needs to be constructed.

In some ways, the narratives about me have been quite good. For me at least. I publish in peer-reviewed journals and conferences. They accept blinded submissions. In other words, they are judged on the quality of my work. The opinions of the twitter trolls come to mean nothing. Such is the point of blinding in academic publications. It is only the quality of one's work that matters. I expect to have around 70 publications for the current year — excluding patents, of course. Such publications will be on mathematics, economics, game theory, law, history, computer science, and epidemiology.

They are some of the topics required to understand Bitcoin and blockchain fully. Like it or not, there is nothing that you can do to stop it, whether you like me or not. Here lies the interesting part.

Back to my dilemma: how to find people, when engaged in the creation of a system that will alter the world, who seek more than short-term gain. People not simply seeking money but rather to alter the fabric of the world in history. I believe I found some. I see it in Calvin, I see it in Jimmy, and I see it in Steve. There are other people I will not dox and call out here, but they exist in the background. Such people understand the long term, and by long term I don't mean 6 to 12 months.

How do you find someone willing to work the next decade?

Over the next 20 years, all of it will become clear. I expect, before my time is through, to publish in the order of 3,000 patents and 5,000 or more peer-reviewed publications. At such a point, it becomes rather difficult to hide. I'm not publishing them pseudonymously or anonymously but rather as myself. I can achieve such an end because of the wonderful team I've finally built to support me and the help I get from external parties to keep much of the problems of life away from me.

There are many who will not see my vision and many more who will not support it, yet it has come too far to stop it. The question is now: how do I find the people we need? More importantly, how do I find people I can trust?

Such is the dilemma that is not posted by the trolls and haters. They love to call me a scammer and say that I won't do what they wish. Honestly, I find it quite funny. You see, it is they who seek from me. I wonder how many of you thought about it, the call for me to prove.

"If Craig Wright does not say that he created Bitcoin and sign and dance and do a jig the way we want, he must be a fraud."

As if it is their adoration that I would seek or want.

In proving to the fools that I can sign a key publicly; I open the next round of attacks. I also enable some people to make a quick pump, gain, and exit. It doesn't interest me.

I don't get any special favours when filing patents because I'm Satoshi.

I don't get any special favours when I'm submitting a paper to an academic blind review in being Satoshi. In fact, they have no idea that I am Craig Wright until they accept my paper.

When I finish my current round of studies and sign up for my next PhD, being Satoshi will gain me nothing.

So, I am going to do things my way. It's a long path. It's a hard path covered with thorny bushes and surrounded by brambles. Yet, it's the one I've chosen. And to me, it's incredibly rewarding. It's one where I will teach governments and institutions about the future.

It's a world where I release what I want as I choose. It's a world where, if you have come to my attention and are doing something wrong, I'm going to target you.

The hardest part of all is understanding that, one day, I'll be put in a position that no other person has ever been in. And from there, I need to choose a path, or road of succession. It's a part of why I study Rome and Marcus Aurelius and Octavius. All things are finite, and in my case, succession is something that needs to be planned carefully. But for the time being, the immediate needs to be planned carefully. It's a path that is going to make me seem like a hard and calloused bastard. It's the only one I can choose.

One thing I have learned is that vigilance matters. Even when bringing something good into the world, one needs to be cognisant of Machiavelli and his Prince. It is not whether people like you—for even the most loved has enemies.

I hold a key, a methodology, and a way to definitively prove, and over time, I will release parts of the story bit by bit. As I do, I will utterly destroy the scammers in the industry. I will bring down the ones seeking to make criminal industries out of Bitcoin and blockchain, and I will alter the path of the industry, and I don't care if you like it—for it's what I'm going to do.

In doing so, I am going to create more wealth than I believe anyone could ever imagine—I certainly cannot. And I'm going to make other people wealthy, in some cases wealthier than they could even imagine. More importantly, other people who are partnered with me I'm going to make immense sums, and here is the rub: they are going to work like they have never worked before.

I don't see anyone getting in and getting out with the sort of gains that happened as the scammers milked people of their money in the past and in the start of the industry.

Because as much as other people want, sometimes for me, sometimes for themselves, a definitive proof, a moment and something they can run with in a bang, there is none. There is a long path where we create a future, a global interconnected world.

BITCOIN VISION

WHAT IS BITCOIN?

We are going to put aside for the moment the issue of hard forks and multiple blockchains, as we will deal with them in the next section. For now, let us focus on what Bitcoin is and what it is intended to do.

There are two types of money. There have only ever been, in human history, two types of money. No one's thought of anything else other than two types of money. Bitcoin does not change this.

One is Fiat. Fiat is by decree. The government says, "this is money because we say you must take it."

Two is commodity. When I tell you, "I can pay you in gold, or grain, or salt, or solarium." Why? Because you're willing to trade it with someone else.

Those are the only ways money has ever worked in human history, and probably the only ways it ever will.

So now, Bitcoin is a commodity ledger. Information has value. Raw data is not information. You add meaning and monetary value to data, and you price it and you get information. People can start understanding it. And that's what Bitcoin is.

Bitcoin is a commodity ledger that allows people to save transactions, save contracts, save proof of existence, save any value, any file, whether it's ASCII art, or eventually any file in a high-centrality global network that no one controls.

Now, no one controls means no one changes. The protocol is really something set in stone. Set in stone is important because if you're trying to build an application on top of money, you don't want money changing. The entire focus of why Bitcoin was really designed was so that you could have a monetary system, a measuring stick that didn't alter over time.

To do that, what commodity do we have? There are bureau services. They do processing for banks. They act like Swift or Visa, and they save data. It's horrible. It's insecure. It's alterable. It's a horrible system.

Bitcoin enables EEI, data transfers, contracting, housing, all sorts of things, utterly securely. Funny enough, most of the lawyers I speak to get it. When you explain the technology behind Bitcoin, those who have a grounding in law and economics start to see the system. Privacy and anonymity are opposites. I am Wesleyan. If you understand that, you'll start to understand my philosophy on wealth. If you read Andrew Carnegie's *The Gospel of Wealth*, (Carnegie 1901) you may start to understand my long-term plans. Unlike Andrew Carnegie, I don't plan to retire in my 50s, nor in my 60s, nor in my 70s, nor even in my 80s.

There is a lot of work remaining to get Bitcoin to where I want it to be. I expect at least 30 years' of work to do so. At that point, I am hoping it will be sufficiently advanced so that others can carry it forward. Having said so, within the year it will be locked with the protocol fixed and the changes removed.

From here, once it is set in stone, it will remain set in stone.

It is simple to say that things should be different. It is difficult to stand up and take the brunt of the attacks that come to one who stands against the status quo. It is simple to say things should be different, but it is incredibly hard to have the courage to stand up and fight for change. There are many ways to seek change in our society.

Bitcoin was designed to scale to create something more than the casino that is finance. It is not the exchange that people called the market that allows growth in the creation of capital but rather the exchange of goods between individuals for consumption.

The path forward is already set in stone. And right now, I don't care whether you believe me. I have my own way of doing things, and most importantly, the first part is to understand that code is not law.

I spent 20 years designing Bitcoin. I started in 1998 and went through more iterations than I can ever hope to imagine and remember before finally coming up with something that worked. Welcome to freedom; it comes through a system that consumes utopians and spits them out. The system within Bitcoin is stronger than you believe, and it was designed to not work in many other ways.

It no longer matters whether you like it; Bitcoin was carefully considered, and no blockchain-based system ever allows you to create the totalitarian utopia that is the ultimate dystopia of a world where code is law and order is crushed in anarchy.

PHASES OF THE BITCOIN SYSTEM

The Bitcoin system may be broken down into the following "phases"
- Mining
- Holding Bitcoin
- Transferring Bitcoin

Each of these phases are discussed in turn below.

Mining

In its May 2013 report to the United States Senate Committee on Finance, the United States Government Accountability Office described the mining process in the following terms:

> Bitcoin are created and entered into circulation through a process, called mining, that members of the Bitcoin network perform. To perform the work of mining, Bitcoin miners download free Bitcoin software that they use to solve complex equations. These equations serve to verify the validity of Bitcoin transactions by grouping several transactions into a block and mathematically proving that the transactions occurred and do not represent double spending of a Bitcoin. When a miner's computer solves an equation, the Bitcoin network accepts the block of transactions as valid and creates 25 new Bitcoin and awards them to the successful miner.

The rate of creation of 12.5 new Bitcoin was current rate at the time of this paper. The Bitcoin algorithm is designed to reduce that rate over time (halving approximately every 4 years). As noted, the mining process involves the Bitcoin network updating a shared public ledger or log on the Bitcoin network:

> The entire network is used to monitor and verify both the creation of new Bitcoin through mining, and the transfer of Bitcoin between users. A log is collectively maintained of all transactions, with every new transaction broadcast across the Bitcoin network. Participating machines communicate to create and agree on updates to the official log. This process, which is computationally intensive, is in fact the process used to mine Bitcoin.

Holding Bitcoin

Each Bitcoin user has a digital wallet known as a "Bitcoin wallet" which incorporates a public/private key pair.

Bitcoin are recorded in the shared public ledger on the Bitcoin network as being under the control of a selected individual Bitcoin wallet and key pair. The wallet and key pair are the only way of accessing the Bitcoin. (Bollen 2013)

As such, Bitcoin are "owned" and "held" by the user who has control of the relevant Bitcoin wallet.

Transferring Bitcoin

A Bitcoin wallet is also how Bitcoin are transferred between users. Specifically, Bitcoin are sent or received from one or more "Bitcoin addresses" associated with a Bitcoin wallet. A Bitcoin address is an alphanumeric string derived from the public key incorporated in a Bitcoin wallet.

The process of transferring a Bitcoin may be summarised as follows:
- the recipient provides their Bitcoin address to the sender
- the sender adds the recipient's Bitcoin address and the quantity of Bitcoin to be transferred to a "transaction" message
- the sender's message is digitally signed by the sender's private key incorporated in the sender's Bitcoin wallet. The sender's public key is also announced to enable verification of the message
- the "transaction" message is broadcast over the Bitcoin network and verified, and the Bitcoin transferred from the sender's address to the recipient's address

Only the first two steps involve action by the sender and recipient. The latter two steps are automatically executed by the Bitcoin software and the Bitcoin network.

Importantly, Bitcoin are transferred directly from the sender to the recipient. Bitcoin "miners" validate and update the transaction in the public ledger but are not payment intermediaries.

A basic Bitcoin transaction may be shown in diagrammatic form as follows:

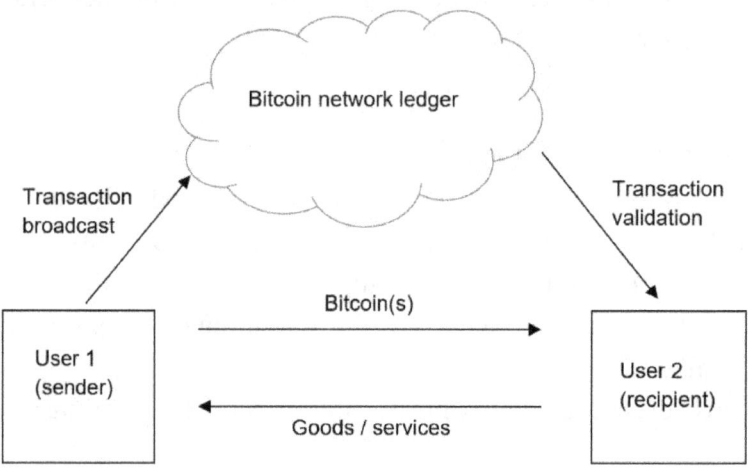

PEER-TO-PEER

Bitcoin is peer-to-peer electronic cash. An exchange in Bitcoin can be made from one party to another directly with no intermediary. The aim of cash is not to have a system where a central bank signs off on the monetary unit, issuing these to third parties such as consumer banks, MasterCard and visa. Rather, it is a hard-stable currency system that allows individuals to exchange directly. In the first version of Bitcoin, there was a rather poorly constructed IP-to-IP protocol that allowed users to exchange keys. The version implemented at the time was not secure and allowed man-in-the-middle attacks. This is something that can be easily fixed, and many protocols exist to solve this now.

In handing a transaction from one party to another the primary concern is that:

> *"Transactions that are computationally impractical to reverse would protect sellers from fraud." (Nakamoto, Bitcoin: A Peer-to-Peer Electronic Cash System 2008)*

This is what peer-to-peer means. Miners are a settlement layer. In the banking system even when money clears into your account it may not settle. Any payment received by a merchant over the credit card system can take 90 days to clear. Banks allow you to access funds, however any reversal can be applied retrospectively placing accounts into arrears and requiring the payment of interest and fines.

This is the difference that makes Bitcoin peer-to-peer. Not that every person needs to be a miner, but that individuals can exchange transactions directly with each other and quickly verify that mining nodes have received the transaction.

USERS ARE NOT MINERS

Much of the problem has come from the myth of the full node. The idea that every user must also be part of a mining network. Users should be running Simplified Payment Verification (SPV.) This is defined within the original white paper. There is no requirement to validate every single transaction.

This is the ease, simplicity, and beauty of Bitcoin. It is not miners that you trust, but their competitive nature. The argument is that miners act in concert as one. They do not. Miners are competitive businesses designed to end in datacentres.

The simple fact is that ease-of-use comes from developing applications on top of Bitcoin, things like the HandCash Wallet App, Keyport, POP, and Centbee—that deliver simplicity—are what matter.

The value of Bitcoin is not the electricity in the system, it is the value in exchange. People are willing to pay for this using electricity in mining. There are no absolutes in the economic world, and this holds true for Bitcoin.

The question to always ask is not whether something uses energy, but rather whether it delivers an outcome that people want more efficiently. Bitcoin delivers the first form of stable money ever developed in human history and it does this at a cost lower than the combined cost of monetary issue, electronic data exchange, and fiat money as they exist today.

As an economic system Bitcoin self-adjusts in mining and fee reward, based on the overall utility of the system. Most importantly, as the system scales it becomes more and more efficient.

At a global scale, the system can operate more effectively than the credit card system alone while delivering far more.

DIGITAL CASH

Bitcoin operates as a financial instrument (Watterson and Zerega 2013). Depending on how the transaction is constructed this can be a contractual exchange, electronic cash, a promissory note or another financial security, a bill of sale, or a simple ledger entry. In each instance, from the creation from the Coinbase allocation of rewards (Bitcoin Wiki 2018) to the payment and consideration for an exchange, many regulatory and financial considerations arise.

The courts have developed many different views concerning the nature of money. At its simplest, however:

> Money is any generally accepted medium of exchange for goods and services and for the payment of debts (see Butterworth's Australian Legal Dictionary at 759). Currency and legal tender are examples of money. However, a thing can be money and can operate as a generally accepted medium and means of exchange, without being legal tender. Thus, bank notes have historically been treated as money, notwithstanding that they were not legal tender. It is common consent and conduct that gives a thing the character of money (see Miller v Race (1758) 1 Burrow 452 at 457). Money is that which passes freely from hand to hand throughout the community in final discharge of debts and full payment for commodities, being accepted equally without reference to the character or credit of the person who offers it and without the intention of the person who receives it to consume it or apply it to any other use than in turn to tender it to others in discharge of debts or payment for commodities (see Moss v Hancock [1899] 2

QB 111 at 116) (Travelex Limited v Commissioner of Taxation 2008)

Being money, Bitcoin is an intangible property that is capable of being owned. What is less clear is if Bitcoin is "currency." However, the acceptance by the German Government of Bitcoin (Clinch 2013) as a unit of account and the postulate before the Swiss Parliament asking that Bitcoin is treated as a foreign currency suggest that Bitcoin may be "currency." If not now, it seems inevitable that Bitcoin will be formally accepted as currency by a government soon.

BITCOIN IS NOT YOUR BANK

There is this myth around banking and Bitcoin. Any quick search will show thousands of sites and people promoting the idea of "be your own bank." This seems to be one of the catchphrases associated with Bitcoin. However, it is utterly false. Holding Bitcoin as cash is not banking. In Japan, due to the low interest rates offered, many people still hide their money under their bed. Just holding your money in Bitcoin is the same as holding your money under your bed. This is not what banks do.

Banks allocate and distribute capital. They offer loans and allow people access to funds they would not be able to gain based on the promise of future repayment. They bail out people who cannot afford a home to buy one and pay it off over time. They allow people who come from poor families to seek education and pay this off later. Bitcoin does not offer this.

It is possible to have banking based on Bitcoin, but it does not involve holding your money at home.

If you have a home loan, try and think what it would be like without access to banks. Imagine, as people used to do, having to share a small room as you save—maybe forever.

One wonderful advantage that Bitcoin provides is that with simple applications such as Centbee and Handcash low-end users can access Bitcoin quickly. In environments where banking is not available Bitcoin partially provides leverage to get into the market. It doesn't provide all that banking does, but that does not stop us from building applications on top of Bitcoin that allow for localised services.

More, Bitcoin provides a means for these people without access to save their money to have some way of doing it. It allows them to have multiple wallets and only carry the minimal amount on their phone. They can have one phone at home with a special backup key and locked encryption and carry another with a minimal amount that they need for the day.

This is the type of thing that should be taught. Yet this is not taught at all.

The so-called experts teach you about the false idea of being your own bank and tell you nothing about how you need to secure nodes.

They do not teach storeowners that the central head office can have a different wallet that is paid into with no private keys on site. They do not teach people being paid for work that they can have multiple keys and multiple wallets storing these so that they carry one with a small amount and get paid to another.

It is time to start teaching people the truth. Bitcoin does not replace banking. It is cash.

Too many people get it wrong. As the white paper explains, Bitcoin is a peer-to-peer electronic cash system. In the white paper, it is written, "costs and payment uncertainties can be avoided in person by using physical currency, but no mechanism exists to make payments over a communications channel without a trusted party." (Nakamoto, Bitcoin: A Peer-to-Peer Electronic Cash System 2008)

There is a reason for it; Bitcoin is an electronic cash system, not a 'crypto' system, and not a currency in any form. I will start detailing the part concerning currency.

WHAT IS CURRENCY?

Black's Law Dictionary defines currency as:

> Coined money and such bank-notes or other paper money as are authorized by law and do in fact circulate from hand to hand as the medium of exchange. (Black 1995)

Alternatively, other terms such as virtual currency have developed. A virtual currency is defined as:

> A digital representation of value that is not available in physical form but which can be used as a medium of exchange, a unit of account, or a store of value. Virtual currency is stored and transacted in electronic form, and therefore does not have legal tender status in any jurisdiction. Virtual currency includes a subset referred to as cryptocurrencies (an example of which is Bitcoin) which are protected by cryptography.

Unfortunately, the errors around what Bitcoin and other things are have propagated, and many people claim that even Bitcoin is a cryptocurrency.

> A subset of virtual currency and digital currency that is protected by cryptography and predominantly generated and exchanged through the use of blockchain. While all digital and most virtual currencies are centralized with supply controlled by the developer of the currency, cryptocurrencies such as Bitcoin are decentralized

and not created or controlled by a single central entity. Therefore, supply and value of cryptocurrency is determined by demand.

As such, they fail to even define the notion of decentralized. Even the description used is logically flawed. Virtual currencies are defined as being centralized because the supply is controlled by the developer of the currency. They write that cryptocurrencies would be different because they were decentralized and thus not controlled by a single entity or group (such as a small group of developers as with Bitcoin Core or Ethereum).

The same by nature reflects a requirement for a set protocol. If any party can alter the protocol, then it is not by nature decentralized and is controlled by a single (usually not incorporated) entity. Importantly, the Fifth Money Laundering Directive ((EU) 2015/849) (MLD5) has already been updated to incorporate all the changes, and unfortunately misuses the terms cryptocurrency within the industry.

Article 1(1) of MLD5 extends the "obliged entities" that fall within the scope of MLD4 in several ways, by amending Article 2 of MLD4.

> *Providers engaged in exchange services between virtual currencies and fiat currencies. Fiat currencies are coins and banknotes that are designated as legal tender and electronic money, of a country, accepted as a medium of exchange in the issuing country, such as the euro. The Commission refers to this type of provider as a virtual currency exchange platform (VCEP).*

Importantly, the MLD5 already calls for provisions to:

> *...combat the risks related to the anonymity, national Financial Intelligence Units (FIUs) should be able to obtain information allowing them to associate virtual currency addresses to the identity of the owner of virtual currency.*

CRYPTO

The confusion stems from the fact that ECDSA, the digital signature scheme used within Bitcoin, has a similar basis as elliptic-curve cryptography or ECC. In fact, public-private key schemes within them are the same and interchangeable. The difference is that Bitcoin is a mere signature. It is sent in clear text. Cryptography is secret writing. Bitcoin is not secret. Unfortunately, here lies the confusion that has become part of the core of the system.

Cryptography simply means secret writing. As explained, many of the mathematical functions used within Bitcoin are like those used within cryptography, but Bitcoin is not cryptographic.

Digital signatures are based on the same mathematics as public-key cryptography. Here's where it ends. Based on does not mean is. A digital signature is a tool that provides a means to validate the authenticity and integrity of any data. It does not provide confidentiality—which is encryption.

E-CURRENCY

Bitcoin is not a currency or an e-currency at present, but it could be. Importantly, tokenisation methods allow for the creation of a national currency on top of Bitcoin. Such a system would be an e-currency.

It is not a lost cause even now, and we have the capability to securely tokenise currency offerings on top of Bitcoin.

Unfortunately, many people have not understood the nature of Bitcoin, currency, or how the system functions. The truth of the matter is, Bitcoin is and was at its heart an electronic cash system that works as a peer-to-peer exchange. It is not because nodes act as peers, but rather individuals do. When Alice and Bob exchange consideration using Bitcoin, Alice sends a transaction to Bob that he can send to the network to be settled. The peer-to-peer process here happens between Alice and Bob and does not involve the network other than in settlement. Too many people have got it wrong.

Far too many people fail to understand what I said. At no point have I said that Bitcoin is a cryptocurrency, a currency in any form, or anything monetary-wise other than digital electronic cash. It is important; there are legislative requirements detailing the handling of currency. The handling of Bitcoin and other electronic systems has now been incorporated into the acts. Having said so, Bitcoin only becomes an e-currency when it is used as a national currency or when it is the basis for any currency that has been built into a script with Bitcoin as a token.

SCALABILITY

This is the biggest myth around Bitcoin, that it cannot scale on chain. The only problem with scalability is the subsidising of home-user hobby nodes. Bitcoin can scale to terabyte size blocks today. The only thing stopping this is a false idea that nodes that do not mine Bitcoin are required in the network. Miners are competitive organisations.

There is one simple reason people have problems with scaling blockchains. They were always designed to be commercial in nature. They were designed to be competitive. And they were designed as a monetary transfer unit. There is one and only one way for Bitcoin, in fact any blockchain, to function successfully; that is as a single unit with a primary focus on cash.

Once this is accepted, the myriad other uses all fall into place. Just as users do not run their own email servers, their own web servers, or any other server farms, Bitcoin uses corporate validation of data not as a trusted third-party, but as a protocol-specific system. It works because capitalism is a system of competition. Bitcoin is purely competition driven. It does not matter whether you like this or not because Bitcoin is apolitical other than being purely capitalist.

The reason we can trust Bitcoin and we can trust miners is the protocol governance mechanism. This works as a monetary unit for the simple fact that there is no such unit as miners.

It is the same as saying the typical comment about suits. There is no one form of corporate executive. How do we trust these corporate entities? Very simple, we trust them to be greedy. Moral sentiments are a layer over and above corporate culture and this doesn't come into the governance of Bitcoin at all. It relies on profit seeking. We know it works as we know that corporations will seek the greatest profit and they will do whatever they can to get this. This is why Bitcoin works. The most efficient organizations will seek an edge over their competitors and in doing so will drive mining profitability to an eventual knife edge. At this point there is no way for any corporate entity to gain any means of altering anything within Bitcoin. To get to this point we need to scale.

The cost of scaling Bitcoin exceeds the cost of network and system architecture. There is no scaling limit. There is no such thing as spam in Bitcoin. Any party willing to pay for a transaction can have that transaction stored. Miners compete to grab as many transactions as they can as this is the way they gain the profitability edge over other miners that is needed to stay competitive. In time, nearly every bit of a miner's profit will come from a transaction.

The truth of the blockchain when done correctly is that there is no scaling ceiling. The more use, the more profit, the better it scales, and the less expensive transactions become. Bitcoin is incentivised to become the backbone system of the global Internet.

SECURITY

For most people, the home is not the safest place. This myth that holding your own keys makes you secure is a fallacy.

There is a monetary cost to maintain a safety deposit box. Any large amount saved within a set of Bitcoin keys is at risk and needs to be protected. This works well if you are wealthy and can afford it, but it is not the same for the average person. Most users are not well-versed in information security. Having worked within information security since the early 90's when most people hadn't even heard of the discipline, I can tell you very well that the biggest security problem is users not understanding security. Handing off security to users is a recipe for failure.

To be safe, you cannot trust a hardware wallet. All devices have a level of insecurity and risk. You need to be able to have multiple layers of security and for any large amount of Bitcoin this includes backups, secure off-line service, and multiple keys. For any large amount of Bitcoin being stored there is a cost of storage associated with maintaining security.

To teach people that Bitcoin is secure by default is negligent.

In the future, I expect people touting this idea to be sued under tortious negligence laws for promotion of false information leading to loss. Those who have trusted in the security of Bitcoin and then had machines hacked, lost information or had keys stolen—even through physical acts—should look to some of these people promoting the lie that owning a set of keys makes you ultimately secure to recover their funds.

PERMANENT IMMUTABLE LEDGER

For security, Bitcoin needs a central ledger. I'd been doing forensic accounting. CAT software is computer-aided audit technology. And with that, I would write programs to find fraud. In public companies we always have some fraud. So, a few people in C-level suites ended up losing jobs because of me a few times, which wasn't always liked.

But from that, I learned the whole small-scale version of Enron and Bernie Madoff. All these firms, when they're doing something wrong, even departments, keep multiple sets of records. And any of the ways people are doing Bitcoin right now and thinking it works allows you to have multiple sets of records still. It's an immutable nothing.

It came down to figuring out that if you want to do this, you need a way to have a single, immutable ledger.

Even with wormdrives—which are write once, read many, which is required under FINRA and S.E.C. rules after 9/11 and Enron—you can still write two copies. I could put in one immutable copy and another immutable copy, and hand you the one that suits what I want to say at the time. So, if I can do that, and I can have multiple records, then I haven't really solved anything. I've given the illusion of having a real order. Auditors are fooled like that.

The only way it really works is if there's one universal copy, if we have a single protocol, like the Internet is a single protocol. If we create a single global protocol that enables everyone to have a defined record. The beginning of the year, you go to the tax authority, the regulator, the SEC, whoever you lodge with, even make a public announcement in an uber-libertarian world. Say, this is my year's record number, that relates to a key, and have a defined set of values that will be your daily account sales. And you can't change it. Then, if you link that in cryptographically you have a way of having one provable source. That no one can ever alter.

Not many people realise this, but that makes it, it goes even beyond cash. It means it's the first accounting system in human history that can be a sole accounting system. There can only be one. There can't be multiple versions. There can't be the, "Here's what I tell everyone, and here's the under-the-table books." One set of accounts.

Bernie Madoff would have been found out twenty years earlier with that. Enron would have never started. If you look at Barings Bank, all these trades. The losses in P & B Barabbas. All these things happened because people can hide their trades and have a false version, that updates records and changes them after the fact. What happens if you stop them doing that?

I liked the quote that someone said about Bitcoin, the truth machine. I'm running with that because that's effectively what it really is: one version of absolute truth. It doesn't mean you have to tell everyone that truth. But you're stuck with it.

The design of a protocol is a function of the system and organisation it is designed to deliver, and it is always an economic function. Bitcoin is first and foremost cash.

Bitcoin is money, and the end goal is to make the protocol as boring as the global plumbing it reflects.

In information security, for all of the news of new attacks, of zero-days and more, it still remains the systems that have not been patched, the applications that we have allowed off a white-list, and poor practice that cause most compromises and breaches.

When we think of critical infrastructure attacks, it is the simply wrong belief that these systems are okay as they are and that these do not need to be patched that leaves them vulnerable. It is the failure to have basic controls and updates, not the growth of new forms of attack that places these systems at risk. This is along the lines of what we need for Bitcoin, to lock the base protocol and then patch and monitor it for any needed change.

Why? As Bitcoin is money and that makes it a form of critical infrastructure.

I have been told that "old attacks" do not matter and that these could never be used to attack anything. This is the problem with the information security industry, and it is a problem in the development of Bitcoin. Old attacks work. New attacks cost money. APT and zero-days are expensive to both create and deploy. They are the proverbial nuclear weapons. Once they are used, they are depleted. They may be used, but the use is extremely controlled and limited. For each of these, there are thousands if not millions of conventional attacks. This is attacks using old vulnerabilities.

Bitcoin needs to be trusted. To ensure that this is the result, it needs to be seen as boring. Banks used to use Greek and Roman frontages. This classical form of architecture was used to convey stability. That is what Bitcoin lacks. We do not need "cool" projects. Developers want these as they help pad their CV. What the world wants, what the market for money wants, this is just boring, stable and sound money. A platform that does not change and can be used with expectations of 20 to 30 years of stability.

To build a platform, you set the system in stone. Sound, stable and predictable. This may seem boring, but this is the ideal. Bitcoin works when most people see it as boring. When it is not cool. When it is simply cash.

With Bitcoin and the various methodologies that I have created extending Bitcoin, we can stop many financial frauds. Most importantly, we radically alter the nature of the system allowing all organisations to be immutably traced through the ultimate evidence trail that both provides privacy and removes many traditional frauds.

It is what those who seek to move everything off-chain want to stop. Once everything moves to being stored on-chain, and once everything can be linked to a single provable record with no alternate copy of a ledger ever being valid and it can be proved instantly, the nature of the accounting industry will be radically altered forever.

The thing many do not see is that only maintaining a single public blockchain allows for the truth. If an organisation can have multiple blockchains, something that is simple to achieve using private blockchains, then there cannot be a definitive truth. The system is not immutable. The solution merely comes to fruition on a public blockchain. That is, Bitcoin as it was intended. When the organisation can control the inputs, it can easily fork and split many versions of the truth. You cannot do so when there is one global ledger. With a single global public ledger, there is a single source of truth.

STABILITY

The nature of Bitcoin is such that once version 0.1 was released, the core design was set in stone for the rest of its lifetime.

This is something people misunderstand. The nature of Bitcoin's competitive system is designed to make stable money. This is the core of how Bitcoin scales. There are aspects of Bitcoin that need to be fixed, they were in the first version, but they did not include the protocol.

To be stable money Bitcoin needs not to change. I say this again. Bitcoin needs to be set in stone to work and to be valuable. Miners will alter and improve on the core software used for mining Bitcoin. They won't do this as a group. They will do it to gain competitive advantages and they will do it without disclosing all the changes they make. This again is a good thing. More efficiency is always good. To be successful, to follow its key mantra, Bitcoin needs to develop into a system that is fixed. Not something that developers think they can play with, because they understand money very little.

It is important for any monetary system to exhibit stability. This is how and why people trust money. They know that in 10 years or 20 years their money will remain the same. Right now, the developers in Core have been altering the protocol drastically which is the antithesis of stability. It is for this reason that myself with my company, nChain, have been working with others such as CoinGeek and yet-unnamed miners to stabilise the Bitcoin protocol with BitcoinSV.

It is profitability that will drive miners to stabilize and maintain the protocol, creating the first form of digital stable money in human history.

The confirmation times within Bitcoin are fast. People confuse confirmation and settlement. A transaction that has not been settled within a block is secure enough. It does not need to be impermeable; it needs to be good enough.

The result of this is a system that is thousands of times more secure at any scale than Visa or MasterCard and can settle in under a second. As the network increases in size and scale the latency on detecting double spends will decrease and the network becomes more secure. The interesting dichotomy with Bitcoin is the more use and the more scale, the more secure it becomes in the lower risk to merchants that is exhibited in the system.

Confirmation time for a transaction within Bitcoin can be completed faster than any currently deployed electronic system. That is more than enough and as it scales it gets better.

Bitcoin was designed from the start to be a form of stable money, that is: it has a set amount, not that you can buy a set quantity of anything with it.

If you alter money, you always change the "rules of the game." You cannot change Bitcoin without subsidising one party and taking from another. Any change is less than a zero-sum game. The party seeking change (may) win, but only and always at the overall expense of the system and most people using it. This is the key problem with fiat as we have it now. This is what Bitcoin was designed to stop.

DISPELLING THE MYTHS

WHAT BITCOIN IS NOT

Now that we've considered what Bitcoin is, it's time to dispel some of the most insidious myths surrounding it. Code is not law. Bitcoin is pseudonymous, not anonymous. Bitcoin is not anarchist, socialist, anti-bank or anti-state, and it is not intended to facilitate crime.

Core (BTC) is not Bitcoin, and neither is Bitcoin Cash (BCH). BitcoinSV is the blockchain that remains true to the original code and is the one and only true Bitcoin. Finally, decentralization is a means, not an end.

These are the misconceptions we must put aside if we are to move forward and build on the foundations we have built.

CODE IS NOT LAW

Code is not law. Those lazy of thought and mind enough to believe that they can abrogate their responsibility to the society they live in deserve all they get. In a democracy, you have the right to seek change. It does not mean people will agree with you. If you don't like the law, work to change it. The great men of history are not great because they sought to throw away the law, they are great as they sought to align it to freedom.

Here is why we have law. You need to prove the source of funds.

The Holy Grail for many people is the creation of a truly anonymous system. With true anonymity and not simply privacy, there would be little to stop the creation of a criminal empire. If you can take badly designed systems, as ransomware is right now, and create something that allows you to sell and transmit without leaving any evidence, you are in a position that some people would kill for.

Ransomware doesn't work terribly well as there are no ways of guaranteeing that the attacker will give you the decryption key. There is no way of provably knowing that it is the attacker who is shaking you down for money or even if they haven't lost it. Right now, if any such scammers create a network that is too large or too efficient, they are traced, and law enforcement will arrest them.

Therefore, some individuals who have been working on unnecessary products such as confidential transactions and anonymity systems like Zcash and Monero have been working on verifiable proofs in smart contracts. When Bitcoin is used, the introduction of AML/KYC controls to exchanges (as the law has started to require, but which was always really part of funding requirements) leaves the use of Bitcoin for ransomware as something to be avoided. So, what they're seeking to do is to create a payment system that can be used in the exchange with something like Bitcoin, but which is more reliable when used for a variety of different crimes — not just ransomware.

When you're dealing with criminals, you instinctively know that you cannot trust them. So how do you make a solution as a criminal that will allow you to implement something like a ransomware infection that provably demonstrates that a payment to the criminal will guarantee that you get your unlock at the same time?

The criminal can go back and forth proving that they can decrypt files and hence that they have the decryption key, but the same process leaves an audit trail that can be used by law enforcement and makes the capture of the criminal more likely.

So, what you need is something like a Schnorr signature and a mixer.

Combined with a key that is conditionally provable, we now have a system that could be extended to allow another system to be created.

Doing so is of course possible in Bitcoin, but the problem with Bitcoin for criminals is that it has an immutable audit trail. If you integrate something like confidential transactions and Schnorr signatures, then you end up with something different. Here is where you come into the touted concept — decentralised and autonomous. You can make a criminal organisation, one that distributes funds and pays members without having to be registered in any country. This allows you to create ransomware that doesn't have operators and has no head on the Hydra.

When they talk about freedom, they are not talking about free society but the freedom to commit crimes.

IT IS NOT ANONYMOUS

Bitcoin is purposely pseudonymous. There is a fine line between privacy and anonymity, and it is a line that cannot be crossed. What few understand is that anonymity is not privacy. Anonymous transactions do not help the average person, they help corrupt governments and criminals. Worse, anonymous systems will never be legally enforceable. This undercuts their key use as monetary systems and as a method of exchanging contracts.

It has always been the sunshine principal that allows us to detect fraud and dishonest dealings. A system of anonymous money allows those in organisations such as Enron to expand operations in a manner that allows them never to be caught. Anonymous money allows governments to buy deals, votes, guns, and more with impunity. It is not anonymity that leads to free and open exchange but pseudonymous and private communications.

Privacy is important but anonymity isn't. Anyone who does not understand this should read Plato's *Ethics*, and in particular, "The Ring of Gyges" from *Book II*.

Anonymity leads to a system where justice is only in the interest of the strong.

Ten years ago, when I created the site and released Bitcoin, I didn't always check who and where I gave credit to. The problem that I never really thought about was that everyone in the space seems to have wanted an anonymous system. The issues created with an anonymous system are exactly what Bitcoin solves. Bitcoin provides pseudonymous transactions and removes anonymity altogether.

The source of the problem goes a long way back as to why any anonymous system won't work. There was a paper done as a quick montage titled "The Unintended Consequences of eCash." (Froomkin 1997) The notion of an anonymous system barely scratches the surface of the issue and others have gone far deeper in tracing and recovery and how this impacts a monetary system.

The bad news, and the author's predictions on why anonymous money will not happen, hold just as true then and now.

Regulators and law enforcement are not going to allow or change the law to remove the legal restrictions and prohibitions on the issuance of anonymous and semi-anonymous cash. What people don't understand is that it ends up restricting rights of speech when you seek an anonymous cash system. The creation of an anonymous rather than pseudonymous system allows for further restrictions as courts can then tie anonymous speech to terrorist money laundering and other nefarious activities.

And anonymous transactions are anything but anonymous. I wrote years ago about web bugs, and the irony in creating an anonymous cash system is that it leads to a profiling system that allows everything you do to be mapped and modelled and opens the regulatory requirements to enact it. If you want privacy, the last thing you want is anonymous money, because anonymous money allows every action to be traced using legally viable methods and law. With anonymous money, government and regulators have methodologies to supplant social media, ISPs, and the entire framework surrounding the system in a manner that allows complete profiling and capturing not only all the use you like to believe is anonymous but in fact everything you do.

In Bitcoin, I didn't create proof of work nor find a manner of getting it to work, as Hal Finney had done so years earlier. I didn't create the constructs such as a Merkle tree or a tree of signatures as was constructed by Lamport in 1979. Bitcoin uses technology to achieve a means of structuring an economic security system.

I didn't create an anonymous system. I created a system that works with logs and within the legal frameworks that exist within the common-law world. I created a form of money that I posit is a sound commodity because it's an informational service and hence an information commodity. A system that scales because of competitive engagement and that has no single point of failure at scale through the fact that organisations compete and seek to maximise profit.

Bitcoin works because corporations fight to integrate enough technology, enough network capacity, and enough infrastructure to ensure that the network is secure and well-connected. Most importantly, many individual miners compete. In either BTC or ETH even now, we see less than 20 nodes on the network. A node is a single instance of a validating entity. Such can be distributed across many machines and take up an entire data centre as I hinted to in 2010, and yet if one of these miners, one of these nodes fails, the profitability for others increases, attracting others to take their place.

In time, I don't expect to see 20 miners. I would expect to see upwards of a thousand. Governments and banks will want to protect their local environment and interests, and it is very likely that each of them will start acting to protect the network as Bitcoin and the Metanet grow to encompass everything we're doing.

The thing that is new with Bitcoin is the move away from anonymity and finding a balance point on the knife edge of pseudonymous transactions. A system that allows privacy and yet simultaneously remains within the aspects of the law, and one that allows practically every country on earth opening traceability for users and the ability to maintain their own information in a manner that has never been achieved before. The true secret of Bitcoin is that it is an immutable and unalterable evidence trial. A system that with identity registration for corporate groups allowing only a single set of corporate books will stop every future Bernie Madoff scenario. It will stop records being altered such as with Enron, and it will radically alter the face of modern accounting.

PSEUDONIMITY

Let us say, for instance, that AnonCoin has been created. It is a more anonymous, private, and secure coin than either Monero or Zcash could ever hope to be.

Now, there are two aspects of the system that we can incorporate into our analysis and thought experiment.
1. There needs to be some manner of on-boarding onto other systems, and such is an exchange.
2. As a blockchain system, it requires nodes. Such nodes act in a distributed consensus.

The overlooked aspect of any blockchain is the requirement for nodes to reach consensus in a provable manner. The primary way of doing so is a proof-of-work system. Parties cannot cheat, and the investment they have made is reflected probabilistically through the results of a proof-of-work system.

Individuals (or organisations) running nodes can split into smaller fragmented units but doing so comes at a cost. Remember, we have a small-world network, and the more exit and entry points a node is required to manage, the greater the cost. There can be benefits for nodes to have exit and entry points in geographically distributed positions. There is a cost in acting as a set of separate players. Through the small-world nature of Bitcoin, it incentivises any attempt to "sybil" the network. Bitcoin is not a proof of work on finding a block solution but rather finding the block solution and ensuring that all others in the node network have your block to work on before anyone else discovers a competing block.

Consequently, Bitcoin is not about finding a block first. It is about distributing a found block.

Now, in our hypothetical AnonCoin, the nodes are distributed, and it is a blockchain. For it to work, it must be a small-world network. Miners are economically incentivised to act within the rules as it is very simple for other miners to discard dissenting players or nodes.

Nodes could attempt to have many entry- and exit-points acting in what seems to be an independent manner. But due to the nature of the system, it only makes them a larger target by increasing their attack space. In a manner of and analogous to my paper analysing the territorial behaviour of botnets, nodes in the AnonCoin network form an economic balance. Too large, and the cost of maintaining the systems becomes prohibitive, too small, and the distribution function for a global system becomes easy to subvert. The equilibrium will depend on the system, the number of nodes, and the value being traded.

In a proof-of-work system, nodes may be able to come and go, but the requirements for power dictate that it ends in large data centers. More importantly, the network consolidation of a small-world network leads to a small number of competitive miners. To be viable, a scaled system cannot be readily moved. The bandwidth necessary to distribute transactions and blocks to all miners directly without going through multiple hops consolidates nodes into large facilities. There can be hundreds of such facilities globally, potentially thousands for a scaled cryptocurrency, but such are not home-user systems. In fact, there is no way to create a system that is secure and globally distributed and to scale it using a blockchain other than a small-world distribution. No matter how it is constructed, a blockchain-based system collapses into a small-world network.

Recognising the small-world distribution is important. Every resilient system needs to be non-brittle. If AnonCoin seeks to be a system that acts outside the law, it is by nature brittle. Bitcoin was designed to ensure privacy and destroy anonymity. It is an important distinction. Anonymity is the realm of cowards and those without courage. It is utterly different to privacy. Private transactions involve individuals and leave traceable records. People can engage in private communications, and yet have no other party know who they are; different to anonymous transactions, each party in a private communication can trace the other one.

The first attack on AnonCoin is the exchange attack. In the US, bearer instruments have been made illegal. In time, the regulators will understand that systems such as AnonCoin and even by extension Zcash and Monero are bearer instruments.

Simply saying that our anonymous coin is illegal makes the exchange of such a coin illegal. Right now, most exchanges are acting outside the law, claiming to be able to trade without a license. The reality is very simple: Blockchain is a clearinghouse system. It does nothing to protect exchanges or to alter the law of transactional exchange, nor does it mitigate or remove the requirements to hold a license.

In time, it will be explicit and well understood, and such an exchange seeking to operate will be shut down or need to operate as a dark market, allowing for the simple seizure of all assets.

The second part here is the requirement for nodes. There is no working system that will scale with billions of nodes. If the USA decided to ban and criminalise AnonCoin (as it arguably already is a bearer instrument), it effectively ends all use of AnonCoin within the USA.

When I designed Bitcoin, I was extremely careful in the node design. At scale, a blockchain is an immutable evidence store that acts in layers. Users can transact as if it was materialised cash and not a dematerialised electronic transfer. On an interesting side note, a lot of the economic design came from the study into alternative financial systems including Islamic jurisprudence, which I learned during my comparative international-law studies. Bitcoin is in fact (صكوك) sukuk in nature. It operates as a depreciating system within the constraints of one of the largest banking formats globally, one that allows smart contracts such as ones that comply with Murabaha, Ijara, Istisna, Musharaka, Istithmar, etc., while simultaneously allowing typical methods of Western finance.

It is allowing an honest banking system that can track and trace all transfers, leaving records and stopping crime.

Going back to our node situation, we have the scenario when nodes must invest. Bitcoin-based systems form a distributed peer architecture that allows peer-to-peer cash between users which is settled on-chain. It's what the nodes do. The nodes are the clearinghouse and settlement system. Such is the primary third party that is replaced. Bitcoin allows even banks to remove settlement functions and to distribute tokenised electronic cash in a manner that doesn't require something such as the BIS or Bank for International Settlements.

With Bitcoin, people have a method of securely storing cash. They can of course also tokenise many other goods and services allowing for more instantaneous, open, and secure trades to occur. It is a system where people cannot lose invoices and where negotiations can be stored permanently.

The authorities can easily determine the requirement for online service providers (OSPs) to handle the filtering of access in the reporting of such access to banned services.

If made illegal (as I argue that AnonCoin already is within the USA), then an associated node is by nature illegal. It no longer matters how much is being transferred or even if the node operator is poor or rich; the simple fact of the matter is that it becomes a criminal act. Some of the methodologies I developed when working on tracing peer-to-peer networks can be used here. Nodes can't hide in Bitcoin, and likewise, any blockchain with a proof-of-stake or any other thing that AnonCoin could possibly contemplate remains the same if it is developed using blockchain technology.

Now, such is the incredibly important part of any blockchain technology: nodes cannot hide. Bitcoin requires that the commercial nodes, the miners, the systems that run the network and not the users are available. They can come and go, but at the end of the day, they need to connect to and become part of the network. For the same reason, they can be detected and easily mapped. The one real problem that cannot be solved in all of it is that Bitcoin requires a stationary end node. If the requirement changes, the economic ability to earn diminishes. More importantly, nodes distribute to known addresses. They form mappings in the creation of an ultra-small world map. It leads to a system that has the centre of the Mandela network acting to ensure ultra-fast consensus.

It is not the 10-minute settlement time but rather at scale milliseconds which secure transactions.

A node cannot operate as a commercial miner through TOR. If it uses a VPN service, it can be traced. The users connecting to the network, the individuals sending payments to merchants, they can maintain a level of anonymity and privacy conducive to the level of exchange that is being conducted. Even if they don't divulge their identity, they can retain an invoice in an immutable form that cannot be exploited by criminal activity. Such is the real promise of Bitcoin. It is the balance between privacy and the need for safety and security whilst giving up neither. It is putting a cost on the tragedy of the commons and ensuring that privacy is valued.

The myth of AnonCoin is that it can operate anonymously. That nodes can operate at scale without being tracked or recorded or blocked. It is not the case. The only way blockchain—the reality being Bitcoin, but for the purposes here I will say any blockchain—can operate is within the existing legal framework. As soon as it divulges and acts without and outside such a framework, it is simple to block. And once the block occurs, the value diminishes.

No system based on proof of work can scale without value and nodes that can act validly within the network structure and within the law. There are other issues with proof of stake, and it can be used in the creation of a criminal system, but I will detail other flaws in time.

At its heart, this is what it's about. I really don't care if you commit a crime or not, if you buy and sell drugs or not, but what I do care about is that you have just left an evidence trail. If you do not like the law, lobby the parliament, become an MP or, if you're in the USA, a congressman or whatever else, and seek to change it. I have zero tolerance for people who think that rebellion is an option in a working society or rebelling for the sake of rebelling. In some societies, rebellion is an option. Bitcoin does not discriminate between government and citizen; it places the same transparency measures on both and seeks to keep both honest.

IT'S NOT ANARCHIST

Many have thought that Bitcoin was in some manner designed to promote anarchy and a stateless society; that concept cannot be further from the truth. Bitcoin was designed to promote the rule of law. It helps create a system where all are equal under the law and sunlight is shone on the corruption that festers in the dark and hidden regions to make it fade into obscurity.

Anarchy is incompatible with liberty, and Bitcoin cannot be anarchist. Anarchists often claim to *be* "libertarian", but this is just a part of their charade designed to help indoctrinate those who have not really studied liberty into the Philosophy of Collectivism.

The ideology of anarchy is rooted in a concept which (falsely) mandates a path to liberty that is initiated with the dismantling of ALL government. This corrosive philosophy instils the lie of a free society only being able to exist when there is NO government whatsoever.

Bitcoin was designed to allow corporations and people to engage with sound government—not to remove government.

IT'S NOT SOCIALIST

I have noted a good number of people hold on to the same common fallacy as was promoted by Marx. Labour is not a goal; it is a means. If labour can be reduced and the level of production increased, it is a good thing. There is an infinite amount of work and hence labour to be distributed. There is and always shall be more labour available than there are people to conduct it. There is no fixed labour pie that needs to be distributed.

The goal is consumption. It is the creation of real wealth; such as products and services that people want. We DO NOT work to work, but rather for what we can obtain. More importantly, we save and invest so we can have more later, that society can fulfil its obligations, and those who save and invest can expect more to be returned in the future.

Yet, it seems to me that many here worship the obstacles over the end. They see increased productivity through advanced technology and processes as a bad thing. Making more work (labour) is simple. Salt the fields and make agriculture far less efficient, become Luddites, and smash the machines. The problem in the equalisation of all people and "fair distribution" of labour is that we end up all being relegated to being equally poor.

Distributing labour just lowers productivity. Yes, there can be more labour, but as there is less output, we all work harder for less, and we all suffer. The fallacy that labour determines value and that there is a fixed amount of work to be done has to end.

The scaling debate did not start in 2015. It started in 2008 before Bitcoin was even released. The debate has been between, "How do we break Bitcoin?" versus Satoshi's Bitcoin. When I built Bitcoin, I always said that it would be commercial in the end. I've been very clear on it the entire time. It is not about decentralisation in some democratised system. That is demagoguery. The aim was to create a stable platform. An evidentiary system that allowed monetary exchange with traceability that acted within the law. I don't fear a corporation or government takeover on a global system, and nor should anyone who is rational. In particular, the technology acts to ensure accurate reporting and accounting within corporate structures. It incorporates everything that is necessary to ensure that corporations are honest.

It is not a scaling debate; it is a Marxist social utopian debate about this idea of a world without law and government. Bitcoin was launched when it was because of the financial crisis. It did not start, and the design was not created, because of the crisis. It started years before, because I wanted to find a means of creating a system that would simplify auditing. When I worked at BDO, I took the idea further, and was involved with the development of computer-aided audit tools (CAATs). I was constantly surprised by the level of fraud and corporate misappropriation within every organisation I ever audited. Most issues were very small and added up to be a material amount.

The launch of Bitcoin occurred when it did not as a response to the global financial crisis but as I was offered a golden handshake and could leave in December 2008 and start working on the project in 2009.

So, I really don't give a rats' whether you like me, whether you believe me, or a damn thing for that matter, because I have the force of law. Satoshi is not a socialist shit show; he is a grumpy, overworked, overeducated bastard! So, get over it, because it's the best you're getting. You know what, we have filed 692 patents. And it's only just beginning, as the results only come to be published years later with the method we are having. In the next five years, I expect to have over 10,000 patents filed.

Such is what Bitcoin is about. It creates global megacorporations. Not little ones like Google, Facebook, Amazon, or Apple. Bitcoin will create corporations that dwarf every organisation in existence in Silicon Valley, and I'm understating.

All the attacks, all the people out there who I spoke to and who told me time and again how Bitcoin was broken, how their socialist idea didn't work with it can go stick their heads up their asses. It works, we are scaling it, and I'm patenting more of the system than you will ever understand.

Bitcoin is an incentive model. As it is written in the white paper: if a greedy attacker can assemble more hash power than all of the honest nodes, the attacker still has to choose between defrauding people or getting paid to validate transactions. It works because the protocol does not change. And it is very specific. The incentive model of a blockchain does not allow a protocol change.

Very simply, any time a new addition is made to the protocol, it splits from the network. All the old systems, all the SPV nodes, all the people using Bitcoin continue on the original protocol. In telling people that they need to update their software so that they have the new protocol, developers are misleading people into switching from Bitcoin to another system. Such is why the 51% attack is not a problem. Even if an attacker gains 51% of the network's hash power, the best they can do is spend their own transactions or those of whom they are involved with a second time. In doing so, they have also left an immutable evidence trail — which is admissible under law.

The system becomes better incentivised over time. With each halving, the incentive is funded with transaction fees more and more. Consequently, it becomes more and more difficult to attack the system. If a greedy attacker assembles a large amount of hash power, enough to take over 51% of the network, and he seeks to change the protocol, what ends up occurring is that he splits off into a new protocol. Both the old and the new system run simultaneously. The problem, though, for the attacker is that transactions do not go through his system. He needs to mislead users into thinking that the new protocol is Bitcoin. It requires that all users change protocols.

It has nothing to do with running home-user nodes. Only miners run nodes as a node creates a block.

Wallets will validate transactions that they receive. A merchant will check that the transaction he is receiving contains all the required details to ensure that it is valid. It is a part of how SPV was designed to work. Consequently, the merchant would need to change protocol. The merchant does not need to validate every single transaction as a node does. He only validates the format of the transaction he has received as payment. He keeps a record of it, a copy, as it is immutable evidence that is admissible in court. It acts as a receipt, an invoice, and more, and allows him to validate on the node network the state of the transaction source and whether any double spending has occurred.

If the merchant detects any double-spend attempt, he will know about it within seconds, and he can detain the person violating the law just as a shop will detain a shoplifter. More importantly, though, there are valid reasons to double-spend. But such transactions will not be completed in such a manner as it is clearly illegal.

Nodes vote not to change the protocol but rather on whether they will build on a given set of transactions. The reason the protocol doesn't change is that it is outside the purview of nodes to alter it. Nodes can choose not to process a form of transaction, and it is enough to make such a decision to effectively stop such a form of transaction from being used for some time. Doing so will not allow the addition of new protocol features.

The effect is that changes to the system such as Segregated Witness in CoreCoin (BTC) create an alternative to Bitcoin. The misleading part of it is that they create an airdrop of the existing network to mislead consumers.

IT'S NOT FOR CRIME

Bitcoin is money designed for Main St. It was not designed to be the Wall-St casino some want, and it certainly was never designed to be the dark alley between them.

Bitcoin is pseudonymous by design. This allows for privacy and excludes anonymity. Privacy is important; it is required to have a working legal system, and Bitcoin—in fact the entire concept of "blockchains"—is a system built on law. In contracts, you have an exchange, and that requires the ability to prove consideration and the ability to record and recover the contract across time and space.

The concept that a few (fools) seem to think adds value to Bitcoin is to alter the protocol and add the ability to create "permission-less" exchanges. What this means in simple terms is:

- Silk road version 2.0
- Bucket shops
- Assassination markets
- Money laundering, for things like people smuggling and sex slavery

The problem comes from Ethereum (ETH) envy. This ends like a group of misguided anarchistic socialists who refuse to work within the bounds of the law wanting to cry at the world and say, "We do not want law, we want to say what the world is like." It is unfortunate that many grown men still act this way.

The existing script in Bitcoin allows Bitcoin to be used as cash. It can be used for legal and illegal use cases, but it has a ledger that can act as evidence in court. In the existing format, without ideas such as Pay To Identity it operates within the legal definition of money and currency.

With the proposed alterations to incorporate OP_CHECKDATASIG it is no longer cash. So, the simple response is that this is an attack on what Bitcoin is. Bitcoin is not about circumventing law. It was never close to being good for this purpose. It is P2P electronic cash, and it works best when used honestly.

Illegal drug markets and betting shops are not legal.

Bitcoin is not, was not, and shall never be "permission-less". In fact, nothing you ever create will be.

The US Supreme Court (in 1906) defined the category of illegal betting operations known as a bucket shop as follows:

> *An establishment, nominally for the transaction of a stock exchange business, or business of similar character, but really for the registration of bets, or wagers, usually for small amounts, on the rise or fall of the prices of stocks, grain, oil, etc., there being no transfer or delivery of the stock or commodities nominally dealt in.*

We also have the decision of the Chicago Board of Trade where a bucket shop is defined as "a place where bets [are] placed on the commodity prices. The bets are not executed as contracts on any legitimate exchange, but rather, a bet is placed on the bucket shop's books." (United States v. Sanders 1988)

And, we have the generally accepted definition of a bucket shop from Senator Pope in 80 Cong. Rec. 8,088 (May 27, 1936):

> [The] method of doing business wherein orders of customers for the purchase or sale of commodities for future delivery, instead of being executed by bonafide purchases and sales with other traders, are simply matched and offset in the soliciting firm's own office and the firm itself takes the opposite side of customers' orders.

In the U.S. this form of "smart contract" forms what is known as "bucketing," and it is expressly forbidden in commodity transactions, 17 C.F.R. § 30.02(d) (1986).

These are defined in criminal law, not just in the U.S. but in most common-law jurisdictions. In effect, the contract is defined to exchange a derivative interest in a security or commodity future. There is no transaction made on any exchange, though.

The New York Times (Peter J. M'Coy, 70, Former U.S. Aide 1958) reported that a bucket shop is simply "an office with facilities for making bets in the form of orders or options based on current exchange prices of securities or commodities, but without any actual buying or selling of the property."

While I won't comment on the business model of any specific company, I can say generally that offering or facilitating a product or activity by way of releasing code onto a blockchain does not absolve any entity or individual from complying with pertinent laws or CFTC regulations.

This means, any miner validating a block with a DSV OP_CODE can be held criminally liable. The use of a DSV smart contract is not even remotely analogous to script. You can build illegal things using script, but there is no easy manner for a miner to determine the nature of a transaction in the existing script.

The miner is in effect a common carrier and thus not liable.

Once you change the system to specifically add a purpose-designed OP_CODE created to facilitate criminal activity, it is a different matter. In this case, the law is very clear, the miners are individually responsible for any and all blocks and can and would be held directly responsible.

I am working on a prosecutors' handbook for all this; right now, misinformation from scammers in the "decentralised" community has led to a large amount of misleading information. We will be ensuring that this is corrected.

Oh, this means, for any blocks that a miner of the BCH(ABC) chain knowingly builds on with DSV, it will result in their liability. DSV is not like cash. A transaction signed with a valid gaming licence could be constructed and, if used in a PKI hierarchy of certificates, associated with licensing regulators, but, if this was the case, there would be no need nor benefit for doing this in Bitcoin.

A miner can of course accept a P2SH-based transaction with a DSV OP_CODE as they cannot be aware of the content. The issue comes if they allow it to be redeemed using DSV. In this, they are now aware.

A base contract with DSV would be instantly flagged by any miner not seeking to explain the facilitation of illegal activities. You see, a contract designed specifically for a purpose is not even remotely close to the exchange of cash or other transactions within Bitcoin today. There are only a few pools, and it is the pool's job to verify the data as miners seek a hash. So, the individual miners are not liable, the pools are. Solo miners would also be in breach, if they accepted a DSV transaction.

> *In China, fraudulent and deceptive business practices may constitute criminal offences under the Criminal Law (1997, last amended 2015), as well as administrative offences under the Anti-Unfair Competition Law (AUCL) (1993), the Advertisement Law (amended in 2015), the Tendering and Bidding Law (2000), the Securities Law (2006, amended in 2013), the Regulation on Futures Trading, (2007, last amended in 2016), and other measures.*

The Chinese Public Security Agency (PSA) (A.K.A. Public Security Bureau (PSB)) and by the public prosecutor agency, the procuratorate are of course the easiest to sell this to. The procuratorate makes charging decisions, and tries cases before the court, which issues verdicts and imposes sentences (including incarceration or criminal fines).

Confiscation of mining equipment is the easy part, but I am certain they will recover funds. One way or another.

I am in no rush.

The statute of limitations on this crime is long and the blockchain never forgets. There is actually a part of me that would like to sit and watch the carnage, but there will always be dishonest parties who will add illegal contracts into Bitcoin. So, it will be interesting to watch justice come to town.

There are laws in the US, UK, and even China and Japan to recover funds that are mined in Bitcoin for knowingly facilitated crime. DSV is not case, so it is not fungible.

The Proceeds of Crime Act 2002 (c.29) (POCA) is an Act of the Parliament of the United Kingdom which provides for the confiscation or civil recovery of the proceeds from crime and contains the principal money laundering legislation in the UK.

It can be recovered.

I am certain the Chinese government will have a good time with all this...

I used to teach law to police and Feds in Australia. So, you can ignore me all you like when I say, I have already put the charge sheets together as a template for the US, UK, and Chinese authorities. It is time to bring Bitcoin from the Wild West to the staid suburbia.

CORE IS NOT BITCOIN

Bitcoin is only decentralised through the protocol. Here lies the nature of decentralisation. Decentralisation of power involves the inability for an individual to take control of the system. In order to ensure it, developers cannot set the rules. The lie that you are being taught by the promoters of an airdrop copy of Bitcoin which trades with a ticker symbol BTC (also known as Core coin) is that the false copy was in any way decentralised. The truth is that the promoters of such a controlled derivative seek to pass off an extremely highly manipulated system as decentralised.

Such is the founding spirit of Bitcoin: it's a system that acts as a protocol of sound money that leaves a traceable evidential record. It is a system that is antithetical to crime. It is a system that is antithetical to anarchy, and it is a system that works within the law and regulations as they have been constructed in the world of common law.

It is important to remember not that it is a decentralised system, but that it is a global distributed database. Additions to the database are created using a fixed protocol — which is the key here; Bitcoin is a non-trust-based system because it has a fixed protocol. As soon as you allow developers to change the protocol, you trust the developers.

Developers are not decentralised. Developers acting within an open-source project act as a system with a benevolent dictator. I left Bitcoin as a project so that I would not be the benevolent dictator. I left to be an absentee dictator. One who set rules in stone. I explained it well, I would have thought, but obviously it went over everyone's head.

The discussion involved people asking about changing the protocol. It was argued that the number of coins and other protocol aspects of Bitcoin would need to be changed. I said categorically that Bitcoin's rules as a protocol are predetermined.

Bitcoin was created as a system "with no central server or trusted parties." Trusted parties are ones such as developers who hold power over the protocol. If a developer can change the rules, they set the rules.

The first thing to realise is that blockchains do not fork in a manner that splits the chain.

Forks occur. Bitcoin was designed such that orphaning blocks would occur. It is not a bad thing; block reorganisations and forks are part of the design of Bitcoin. An orphan block is a game-theoretic signalling device. To the user, it's irrelevant.

When a dishonest system like Core coin (BTC) seeks to alter Bitcoin in creating an airdrop that poses as if it was Bitcoin, they are conducting an attack on the system. There is a common law tort for it: it is called passing off—which is where someone fraudulently pretends to be someone or something he is not. When Core forked Bitcoin in 2017, they created a new system, and yet they pretend that it was the original Bitcoin protocol. To be honest, to act within the law, Core would need to call it something else.

They could call it Core coin, developer coin, protocol-changes-weekly coin, but they cannot legally decide to name it Bitcoin. They could call it airdrop-altered-version-of-Bitcoin coin and still be honest, but they wouldn't want to do so. They want to pass off their illegitimate copy as the original.

Where such a thing has happened, the reality is the creation of a new system that differs from the original, and if it does not actively inform consumers that it is not the original, it is fraudulently passing itself off as something it is a mere copy of. We see it in Core coin (BTC). Core coin implemented radical changes to the Bitcoin protocol, and instead of launching as a new system, defrauded consumers in leading them to believe that they had bitcoin.

If you simply want to create a copy of Bitcoin, the copyright allows you to do so. You can for instance create a system such as Ethereum or even Litecoin without any risk of passing off and having people confuse your new coin with Bitcoin. It allows for fair and honest competition. But of course, it is not what people in such camps want. They don't want honest competition; they want to use lies and fraud and argue that fraud was somehow part of a libertarian ideal. It is not.

As soon as you allow any developer to start changing rules, Bitcoin is no longer decentralised, and if it is no longer decentralised, it is no longer Bitcoin. I will say it in another way: if the rules of Bitcoin that form the protocol change, you have altered Bitcoin and created something other than Bitcoin.

Just like a SunOS machine from the 80s being able to access the Internet today, to be Bitcoin, the system needs to be stable, and a transaction signed today needs to be valid 50 years from now. If such is not the case, if developers can alter the protocol, you are not talking about Bitcoin.

The big error here is thinking that Bitcoin without government does anything. Without government, Bitcoin doesn't stop banking fraud and doesn't stop fraud at all. Fraud is stopped when you have requirements to act under law and Bitcoin as an evidentiary trail. The point is, Bitcoin reduces the need for certain governmental controls when government exists.

Central banks are not the issue; manipulation is.

> The root problem with conventional currency is all the trust that's required to make it work. The central bank must be trusted not to debase the currency, but the history of fiat currencies is full of breaches of that trust. Banks must be trusted to hold our money and transfer it electronically, but they lend it out in waves of credit bubbles with barely a fraction in reserve. (Nakamoto, Bitcoin open source implementation of P2P currency 2009)

My profound distrust is not towards central banks. It is towards technocrats who think they know far more than everyone else. It is my motivation behind creating Bitcoin. In the quote above, I make it very clear that I do not believe in the long-term viability of currencies that are trust based—that is, the developers can alter them as and when they please! That is, BTC is the reason Bitcoin exists. Bitcoin exists to ensure systems like BTC fail.

There are those out there who try to explain how Bitcoin is about censorship resistance. Primarily, the same people are associated with the fraudulent scam BTC— that is, the airdrop-altered fork of Bitcoin code designed to confuse the ignorant investor.

BTC was eroded the first time a "soft fork" was allowed. There are no forks in Bitcoin. The security of Bitcoin is based on a stable protocol.

As I explained when I wrote the white paper:

> If a greedy attacker is able to assemble more CPU power than all the honest nodes, he would have to choose between using it to defraud people by stealing back his payments or using it to generate new coins. He ought to find it more profitable to play by the rules, such rules that favour him with more new coins than

> everyone else combined, than to undermine the system and the validity of his own wealth. (Nakamoto, Bitcoin: A Peer-to-Peer Electronic Cash System 2008)

Importantly, when we consider an attacker with more hash power in Bitcoin, even if the attacker manages to accomplish gathering more than 50% of the network (by mining hash power) under his control,

> it does not throw the system open to arbitrary changes, such as creating value out of thin air or taking money that never belonged to the attacker. Nodes are not going to accept an invalid transaction as payment, and honest nodes will never accept a block containing them. An attacker can only try to change one of his own transactions to take back money he recently spent.

No node in the Bitcoin network, no miner nor merchant, and certainly no SPV system will accept an arbitrary change. The protocol is set in stone.

The only way that Bitcoin can express censorship resistance is to have a stable protocol. With a stable protocol, what may be temporarily censored today, for whatever reason, can always be replayed later.

Changes to the protocol leave transactions that are already on the blockchain to be marooned in a way that they cannot be later spent. For instance, if a transaction is incorporated into the blockchain using an opcode that is currently valid but which is later considered not to be valid, the transaction cannot be parsed by miners until the payment receipt is sent, which may occur at a time after a soft fork has already invalidated the contents of the transaction.

For a transaction to be censorship-resistant, it must be able to be replayed now and in the future.

If you change the protocol, you can't make the same promise. So BTC is full of censorship. Consequently, BTC is not Bitcoin, and is all about censorship. Every time you change the protocol, you censor a transaction. There is no way to tell which transactions may or may not be valid anymore because of the addition of pay to script hash (P2SH), and worse, SegWit means that you cannot determine the format of signatures or opcodes that may be there in the future.

Bitcoin doesn't change protocol. It is why we will fix the errors in bad code that has been introduced into Bitcoin and then ensure that the protocol is locked down and set in stone as it was designed to be.

Bitcoin BTC, core coin, whatever you want to call it, is not Bitcoin. I say that quite openly, because it is not peer to peer. Miners are not peer to peer. Peer to peer, as I've said before is you and I doing a transaction, and those guys over there making sure it happens. That's what peer to peer is.

CASH IS NOT BITCOIN

There is a lot of misunderstanding on how money works. Many in the Bitcoin space think that scarcity of Bitcoin alone determines the price of Bitcoin. This is utterly misguided and wrong.

The total money supply is not only Bitcoin, but all money. If there is a substitute, then this is a part of the money supply. The scarcity of Bitcoin to price is a function of use.

In economics, this was the issue that Ricardo and Marx never grasped, that is, the diamond/water paradox. The fact that something is scarce is not enough to make it valuable. There are small vineyards who produce under 1% of the amount of wine made by Moet and yet, some of these earn under 0.75 Euro a bottle. Clearly, being scarce does not help increase the price of something that has little use.

This is the issue few understand with money. It is not the fact that a token is scarce, it is the fact that it is in demand at the margin. For this, it needs use.

The value of money in not as a type of money, but in its use when compared to alternatives. For Bitcoin, this is fiat, other coins, and more. In this post, I shall limit this, *ceteris paribus* to a market of only two options. We will have Bitcoin and WormHole Coin and start with just Bitcoin.

We have a limit of just under 21 million Bitcoin. The price is determined in the use at market. Where this is first an issue is that the market is "Main Street" and is not "Wall Street." Speculation adds to the volatility, and is necessary in any system, but like all things, it is not the entirety and the real value of a system, the long-term value and liquidity of a system come in use and circulation.

In this, if we have 11 million coins saved, the value to the market comes from the 10 million in active use. Money measures the demand for goods and services as are available at the time. If the total money supply is 21 million and only 10 million are active, the 11 million have some effect in the fact that these will come into circulation when the demand changes the rate of exchange such that the savers enter the market and exchange the money they saved to receive goods and services.

So, taking the 10 million Bitcoins in circulation, if 10 million Bitcoins buys 10 million ounces of gold (and we have the 11 million BCH locked up to simplify this explanation in a time-locked savings), we have a set rate for exchange, all things equal.

Now, let us consider two scenarios.

Scenario 1.

We have 1 million Bitcoins lost suddenly from the 10 million in active use. This leaves only 9 million Bitcoins that are chasing 10 million ounces of gold.

Originally, we start with a ratio of 1 BCH to 1 ounce XAU.

Now, after the loss, we have 9 BCH to 10 ounces XAU. The loss has resulted in the exchange value of Bitcoin (BCH) increasing, and those who have access to readily exchanged Bitcoins have an increase of 11.1% in the exchange value of Bitcoin to gold. The loss of Bitcoin from some parties has increased the value of Bitcoin owned.

Scenario 2.
We now consider the entire amounts. If the Bitcoins in circulation is only as a result of the market, and not as they are locked and can be moved, then, the increase of value will result in some Bitcoin moving from savings to use.

Let us assume that the holders of 1 million of the 11 million in saved Bitcoin now see gold as more valuable. We now have a value at the margin that will equilibrate to allow a gain of somewhere between >1.00 and <1.111 times the original example.

The reason for this is that some Bitcoin will now seek to realise the gains.

Overall, the loss has a positive impact on the price of Bitcoin compared to gold.

Burning Bitcoin to another system
In an alternate scenario, we will contrast losing Bitcoin with "burning" Bitcoin. In this instance, we have the same amounts of gold and Bitcoin with the same ratios. The distinction is that in place of "losing" the keys and Bitcoin, we have a (perceived) "backing" of WHC in an exchange. That is, for every BCH you exchange, one hundred WHC is provided in a one-way transaction.

Now, let us reconsider the two scenarios.

Scenario 1
We have 1 million Bitcoins burnt in exchange for 100 million WHC suddenly from the 10 million Bitcoins in active use. This leaves only 9 million Bitcoins. However, we also have 100 million WHC used as "money." As such, we have 9 million BCH plus 100 million WHC that are chasing 10 million ounces of gold. Let us simplify this by calling 100 WHC as 1 WHC*.

Originally, we start with a ratio of 1 BCH to 1 ounce XAU.

Now, after the "burn", we have 9 BCH PLUS 1 WHC to 10 ounces XAU.

The burn has resulted in the exchange value of Bitcoin (BCH) and WHC* remaining nominally the same. The entire supply of Bitcoin is reduced, BUT the supply of money has not changed, it has simply been altered to now include a mix of BCH and WHC.

We have 10 units (9 BCH units plus 1 WHC unit) for each XAU.

The difference is that as we lose BCH, the ability to trade in BCH decreases as the ability to trade in WHC increases.

Scenario 2

We now consider the total, and see that as no value has changed, the saved BCH do not matter in the calculation. Those who hold BCH have gained nothing as WHC slowly (and insidiously) replaces Bitcoin with a proof of stake (PoS).

Burning Bitcoin in exchange for another token cannot be compared to losing access to keys.

THE SCAM

The scam is that the WHC address is not a true burn address, which itself is bad enough. The WHC address is a real BCH address that will be able to be "found," if the initial fraud does not work. This of course could also be used as an "Oh, Bitcoin is not secure, move to WHC sham."

The primary difference here is that we are assuming a set ratio in the market of WHC. The truth is far different. Once the quantity of BCH is expended, WHC as a PoS system controlled by Bitmain can simply issue more WHC. There is no way to stop this, it is not a set and limited system such as Bitcoin is designed to be.

WHC is in effect digital fiat. Once you have been drawn into the sham, the majority holders can just add more and more WHC. Users are forced to use WHC in the issue of other tokens and this returns to Bitmain.

The scarcity of the system is only one aspect of value. The real determination of value is in use. That is not HODL and exchange scams, but use as cash, use in a ledger unit, and any other use that people pay for.

PERMISSION-LESS.

The simple fact is that all items in the real world are subject to law. It does not matter that your tokens infer that you own an item. If a court assigns ownership of an underlying asset, the ownership of the asset is moved. There are no ifs, no buts, and no maybes. The word of the court is law. Courts interpret statutes enacted by legislatures or common law. If you have a property, and you lose a court case over the ownership of that property, it does not matter one bit whether you have a token assigning control to you.

If you have digital locks and these are tied to your token, you will need to hand over the token. If you fail to do so you are in breach and hence contempt of court. A contempt of court charge brings unlimited incarceration. A judge can incarcerate you until you comply. The result of this is that you either hand over the token or become subject to law.

It does not matter whether you are in the jurisdiction of the court. The property will be transferred without you. Any other property you also have can be seized and transferred by the court to make up the value if there is any damage in changing the lock from the token. If it is a share or an equity, this will simply be assigned away from you to the winning party.

If you don't like this, welcome to the real world, too bad. This is not a matter of arguing with me, it is pure existence and the world you live in. If you don't like it, vote against it, at least if you live in a democracy.

In simple terms, it does not matter whether you want to issue a token that you call permission-less. Any token that breaches law and the jurisdiction of a court will become instantly worthless. As soon as your token defies the national law where the property it seeks to cover is located, that entire system will be in breach. The result is that any property associated with that token will become instantly able to be attacked and the value of the token itself will become worthless. The owners will have to expend money to prove ownership outside of the token system mitigating any benefit that you advertise.

At best, this results in a fraudulent misrepresentation and anyone with the token has a right to sue the issuers. We can expect many class-action suits in coming years.

OMNI AND WHC DO NOT REQUIRE BITCOIN

They do in one sense—WHC uses Bitcoin in the same manner a Vampire uses the host. It consumes it.

Nodes in Wormhole sit as a separate layer using a separate token from Bitcoin. They do not require Bitcoin at all, they require time stamping and an ordering system. To work, any system that allows for the time stamping of blocks is enough. It sits above Bitcoin and is not Bitcoin.

The problem with Omni comes from reordering. Any Omni-based system is subject to attacks either as zero conf attacks or if blocks are reordered through orphaning. This is not a problem for Bitcoin; orphans and reordering are the natural state within Bitcoin. These are how miners signal.

Wormhole and Plasma are simply the next stage in a vain attempt to create a system that is not based on Proof of Work. To do this, Bitmain and those working on the Plasma Protocol seek, as they did with Lightning, to create an alternate system that sits parasitically on top of Bitcoin.

What is more fun is that it is incredibly simple to cause problems to the Omni protocol and the parasite layer nodes. Eventually, I shall be writing up a list of security vulnerabilities and attack strategies for Wormhole. Mine is simple, we will build up hash power and stop all changes that people seek to the Bitcoin protocol to allow these parasites. There will be no Lightning Network, no Plasma and no way to make Wormhole work effectively using Bitcoin Cash.

Omni and hence Wormhole suffers from a few major vulnerabilities that come because of the following points:
- block re-orgs destroy the security of Omni and hence Wormhole
- Omni and Wormhole have no zero-conf protections
- being able to quickly order transactions allows Wormhole-based systems to check for the reordering of transactions

All these points are important for Wormhole whereas they are not important for Bitcoin. Bitcoin signals using orphans. When a transaction is sent to the network and the miners incorporate this into two separate blocks that are solved at around the same time leading to an orphaning of one of those blocks, the original transaction remains unaffected.

In Bitcoin, miners care about orphans as it is a loss of profit every time they are orphaned. The users of the system, however, should not care.

The nature of a permission-less system is not what is being sold.

To be permission-less, development needs to occur in a manner that does not require being bound and answering to other parties. Developments within Wormhole are completely permissioned. Any proof of stake system is by nature permissioned.

The way to create a system of money that operates in a permission-less fashion is simple, lock the BCH protocol and build upon it. Bitcoin Cash will remove the various caps allowing people to build within script. They will build wallets and applications and oracles, and all sorts of new systems and they will do this without having to ask the permission of Core developers, companies such as Bitmain, or any implementation developer at all.

That, and only that, is what a permission-less system is.

GAS

WHC "smart contracts" provide nothing that Bitcoin did not have natively in 2009 (Contract Definition 2019). Many do not understand the power of just a few Opcodes. In an interview, Clemens Lay explains a token system that he is releasing in Bitcoin script that does not require separate nodes. (Bitcoin.com 2018)

The concept is that BCH and ETH are merged with Solidity as the language. (Daily 2018)

And, this is from BCH being consumed.

The side effect of this is that WHC is used as GAS and BCH is burnt to make more WHC. This however does not push the price of BCH up as BCH is not essential and WHC can move to BTC and consume it once BCH is destroyed.

As one BCH token returns 100 WHC, if the value of a single WHC ever reaches more than 1% of a BCH, then, it is in the BCH holders' economic interest to exchange a BCH for 100 WHC.

Let us, for example, say that BCH is trading at $600 USD and a WHC is trading at $6.25 USD. You own 50 BCH.

If you sell your 50 BCH to gain the 5,000 WHC—as any arbitrager will immediately do—you now have $6.25 x 5,000 value in WHC. That is, $31,250 or a $ 1,250 USD profit. The 50 BCH would exchange to USD for $30,000. But as a swap, your 50 BCH become 5,000 (50x 100 WHC). 5,000 x $6.25 USD = $31,250. So, a $1,250 gain.

You could immediately trade this for BCH if you wanted BCH and have more and this will continue until the price equalises. The issue is that BCH is being forced down in value in this exchange. As more and more BCH is burnt, there is less on the market.

BCH has no value as a mere digital asset, it has value as cash, so, with the supply retarded, the value of BCH decreases more and more until all we have is WHC, which then moves on to leech off BTC and other PoW coins one by one.

Why would WHC go up?

The changes in progress add value to WHC and reduce the value of cash.

Money is not made more valuable as there is less of it. So, the HODL myth will not add value. If BCH is altered to make WHC function, the aim is to destroy BCH. WHC is not cash, it is a doppelganger designed to take the life from BCH and then move on to the next victim.

Watch out for the WHC coin snatchers

One thing to consider:

"The best way to burn BCH is to send them to OP_RETURN output, it can be pruned and therefore does not put unnecessary burden on nodes."

The way that Bitmain seeks to send BCH to a possible, "Theft address" posing as a burn address also increases the UTXO set. So, they are actively sending transactions that do nothing good and yet burden nodes forcing them to increase the amount of memory required and at the same time are not scaling BCH.

The best way is not to burn — as you do not peg anything by destroying it.

CORRECTING MISTAKES

THERE CAN BE ONLY ONE

When I wrote that Bitcoin was set in stone, I was referring to a protocol that can do about everything and will result in massive damage to the network when split. More importantly, the concept of splitting a digital currency is really scammy. There are no splits, there is a demerger process when all nodes agree, and where they don't, there is the original protocol.

The creation of a protocol change is the creation of a completely new cryptocurrency.

You can airdrop all you like, except it is covered under existing law. Bitcoin remains the original currency that was formed in 2009, and the new currency is created alongside it. There is no democratic voting within money.

Gold was valuable when it was used as a global form of exchange. It was not valuable because gold was different in different countries nor because different governments exchanged at different rates. It was valuable as it allowed a universal measurement of value. Even when individual governments debased the currency, gold was valuable as it allowed measurement of the debasement. And that's important; looking across global trade and global exchange, we want a system of value that can report on debasements and allow us to see the value of our money in any location as it is spent in the location. To do so, we need a stable base currency.

Miners can choose to reject blocks, such as of those that have more transactions than they're willing to build upon. They can choose to risk being orphaned and to orphan others. It is a part of how Bitcoin works. What is not a part of the system is the addition of new opcodes and the radical changing and alteration of the signature system such as with the removal of signatures in SegWit.

All of the divisive and socialist bull about money is at the heart of the attack on miners. With the push towards Proof of Stake, we see that most such myths are nothing but an attempt to create a system that allows for illegal bucket shops, criminal activity, and more importantly, pyramid and Ponzi schemes designed to allow one to facilitate the creation of ICOs which are merely a new form of stealing money. Rather, I should say they are an old form of stealing money with a new label, for none of it is new, and USENET scams existed way back.

To put it simply, there are no forks in Bitcoin. The radical alteration of the base protocol by BTC in 2017 was not an alteration to Bitcoin. It was the creation of a completely new system that simply copied the existing coin holders and ledger and modified the underlying protocol.

Bitcoin is not a consensus system based on democratic voting.

Bitcoin does not democratize shareholding. Shares have been dematerialised for a long time. Electronic trading is nothing new. Being able to create shares outside of a registered body is an old fraud, and it has been going on since the 1960s.

There are absolutely no benefits to society in having many blockchains. First, there are no such things as special-purpose blockchains in the same way that there is no such thing as a special-purpose Internet. You have a general-purpose system that does everything, or you have nothing of value. More importantly, the system security is incredibly low unless it congeals into a single unit and stays that way.

Bitcoin can be used for tokens. It is nothing new.

When you have an equity or share that is created across multiple ledgers, you no longer have a ledger with any value. If you split and make a copy of a blockchain, then you have the original share held on the ledger, and you have a sham copy of the same on another one. As an example, if we have Bitcoin with tokenised gold issued and someone creates a new copy of a blockchain using the original Bitcoin ledger, then we do not gain any further gold. You also cannot now distribute the same gold between two sets of blockchains.

The entire creation of the concept of splits is simply a form of fooling those who have no idea about Bitcoin into believing that you can change the protocol and still have a monetary system that works.

They are attempting simply to take the network effect of Bitcoin and steal it into their experiment. Luckily, we have enough capital now to be able to patent my ideas. Bitcoin, every blockchain that could possibly ever compete with it, and every other distributed ledger technology compete, and only one will win. None of that fazes me because I'm about two decades ahead of the market. I'm very happy to be here, and I don't really care if you wish to ignore me because you don't cost me money.

There is value in being able to withhold information. Information is a commodity. This is the core of the heart of Bitcoin. I have information of value and others want it. Information is property, and I choose how I distribute my property.

One of the worst things within the cryptocurrency space is the community. The toxic rabble that you like to call crypto as a community scares off business and adoption. Do I want followers? No. Do I need followers? No.

I have more intellectual property patented than any bank, any large vendor, and in fact more than even China combined. Very simply, we hit the filing of just under 700 this month, and that alone is only the ones that you will see for now. Unlike most organisations, we hide the publication of our patents as long as possible. It still gives us the priority date and ensures that no one catches on to what we are doing before it is too late—and we will have moved on to the next 20 projects.

With just under 1,200 white papers that in time will lead to around 10,000 global patent filings, I really don't give a shit whether you like what I'm doing. But you are going to have to pay attention whether you like it or not.

Bitcoin doesn't create equality, no blockchain does. The existence of a sound commodity money based on principles of supply and demand does not mean you become richer, and it does not mean that local currencies alter in form. It does mean that they compete, and it requires far more than simply having Bitcoin as a HODL platform, in other words a pyramid scheme or Ponzi.

What Bitcoin adds is efficiency. It does not democratize shareholding, and nor should it. Like it or not, people can issue shares in companies, and governments can control them however they want. Regulations are designed to protect investors. The interesting thing is that investors seek capital that is better protected. There is a premium placed on investing on the New York Stock Exchange over the Delaware exchange. The reason is simple: investor's confidence.

With global corporations, a company in California can seek to raise money through the issue of shares on a stock market in Panama today. With de-materialisation, the electronic trading and payment are quick and simple. For the consumer, existing broker systems are more attractive than any digital token right now. It is not the consumer that is seeking the technology.

One party to the problem is the capital raiser seeking to gain a benefit without going through the necessary consumer protections. Right now, there are many ways of raising money from sophisticated investors. Such is the real issue with ICOs, and the fraud propagated in selling them as democratising finance. They are democratising nothing; they are doing the same scams that we saw with pink sheets and USENET tokens over the previous decades ending in the last century.

All of them are seeking to raise money based on the token itself. They are not selling the benefits of the company, rather they are seeking to create a pyramid scheme where they sell the concept of a token that will naturally increase in price because everyone wants it. A monetised and marketed greater fool scheme. The worst of them are scams that offer nothing new to the market but sell a false promise of a blockchain implementation without a blockchain.

The promise of Bitcoin and blockchain is linked to the immutable ledger. It comes when there is one set of books. If an organisation can have multiple sets of books, they can easily commit fraud. If they have multiple blockchains, they can easily commit fraud. As soon as you can start moving between Bitcoin and some sidechain or alternate chain, you can construct elaborate schemes such as those run by Bernie Madoff and Enron. With Bitcoin, vigilance is still necessary, but it is possible to construct a fully auditable system that allows for a single, immutable record stream making fraud more difficult. Not impossible, but more difficult.

ORPHANS ARE A PART OF THE PROTOCOL

I always saw how things would end up in data centres. It is part of the design. Bitcoin is about competitive corporations securing the network. It is not decentralisation for the sake of it, nor is it the creation of a system that removes all government and corporations. Such a utopian perspective is rather delusional.

The security model of Bitcoin is economic, and the cost of running a node was something that I understood and that I think many people did not. Nodes are miners, and such is how they make money. There is no such thing as a validating node. Validation is done through the creation of blocks.

What people fail to understand is that Bitcoin is designed as a commercial system.

True, when it first came out, it was an Alpha product, and the code standard was limited. I am not the coding God that people make me out to be, and there was a lot of work in getting it where it had to be just to launch. More, it didn't even work at first. Bear and Hal acted freely, and gave a lot of advice, and basically fixed a lot of the shit that I had left. I act on a high level these days—Steve and the team wouldn't let me near live code again, and I'm not saying it's a bad thing. It's the curse of being a generalist rather than a specialist.

Nodes need orphans. There is nothing to solve here.

Orphans are an economic signalling technique in Bitcoin. One of the reasons the block cap was put in place is that I did not have a clue how we could have a floating limit work at the time. The problem was that the solutions all required monetary value.

Even orphaning blocks (as a signalling method) requires value to be of use. If you're merely losing a reward of 50 Bitcoin when Bitcoin is not even worth a fraction of a cent, the incentives do not exist to think about the network, the connectivity of your node, or any of the other aspects of Bitcoin that people seem to ignore. This is the point; Bitcoin mining is not about finding a block, it is about ensuring that all other mining nodes know that you have found a block and that it is valid.

Once the network is large, there is an incentive for nodes to watch the validation times and propagation rates of blocks across the network. Once this occurs, they can start monitoring the time of discovery versus the time of propagation for blocks and then set limits on what they will produce versus what they will build on.

A block limit should be an economic function. More importantly, it is more about the inclusion of any transaction that you can take with any amount of fees. Where a miner starts to see orphans occur, they know that in losing the blocks they are losing rewards.

Bitcoin was designed with a two-week limit on difficulty for this reason.

Every 2016 blocks, Bitcoin was designed to reset its difficulty such that the system maintained itself in a fluctuating zero-sum game. It is a multi-leader Stackelberg game. But more importantly, the block reward is a zero-sum game meaning that orphans are not included in the two-week total. For the total supply, the two-week average creation rate will stay at 2016 block subsidies. If there are 1 million orphans, there will still be 2016 blocks discovered. Yes, I am exaggerating there a little, but the point is that extra blocks skew the reward towards better connected networks. Not home systems, but large well-connected data farms that act to ensure that they are incredibly well connected.

The way it works is that if you have three nodes (yes, I know that such is not the case, nor shall it be) for our toy model of Bitcoin and each has equal hash power, then the better-connected node wins more blocks. Imagine two of the three nodes have 10 times the bandwidth of the other. What will occur is that more transactions will be able to be taken and processed by the two miners than by the third on the more limited network. A part of the problem here stems from the block subsidy. People using it as the value of Bitcoin and not as an incentive to build the network as it was intended.

We will assume that a 1GB block can be propagated from the first two nodes without too much problem and that it takes a large amount of time which effectively reduces the comparative hash rate of the third node. If we take block propagation of the 1GB block to take one minute on average (which is excessive but designed to make my point) for the two faster nodes, then each will lose 10% of the hash rate equally. That is, some will gain a benefit, and some will lose but at equal rates. Conversely, our slow node will lose around 65–70% of its effective hash rate.

Instead of an expected daily return of 48 blocks, the slow node will now expect to earn from a mere reap of 16 blocks with the other faster nodes each getting paid an additional 16 blocks in total reward. This is a significant differential and will lead to a scenario where the slow system either goes bankrupt or updates its network. If it was to update its network, the equivalent hash rate between the systems would again equalise. Conversely, if the system went bankrupt, we would expect other players to come into the market due to the large increased profit margins of the remaining players.

On the other hand, if the two nodes can only handle blocks up to 100MB, the node creating 1GB blocks will end up losing an effective 50% of its hash power. This means that it would expect to earn only 24 of the 48 blocks that it is finding each day. The fast node will benefit by slowing down a little, maybe to 300 MB. Doing so will still give it an advantage and yet stop the losses from having the main impact.

Most importantly, as the block subsidies start to disappear, more and more of the profit-earning capability of a node will need to be derived from transactions. To do so, a node will want to build more and more transactions into a block. The issue now becomes one of paid versus unpaid transactions and of a rate per transaction.

There is no need to create an artificial fee market.

The socialist fools of Core don't understand that markets don't need their help. They seem to believe that they need to be the socialist planner saving the Utopia that they wish to create. It is the irony of them calling themselves libertarian.

Orphans are the signalling method that allows organizations to control the rate of discovery and the rate of loss in a manner that lets them know when they need to upgrade their network and also to control the fee level that they will take. There should always be a certain number of free transactions in every block. Fees should be driven to a point that is as low as possible, and through capitalist competition should be driven so low that inefficient nodes are bankrupted and removed.

Subsidising home users removes the security of Bitcoin and allows it to be easily attacked. Bitcoin becomes secure because many competing organisations fight for the right to take your transaction.

There is nothing to fix in orphans. They are a critical part of the design of Bitcoin.

FIXING THE PROTOCOL

One of the flaws in the mangled version of Bitcoin we have today comes from the ability to "burn" and destroy coins. Bitcoin was designed as stable money. This is a fixed-token money system where the cap is maintained in time and fees are used to reward miners.

> Total circulation will be 21,000,000 coins. It'll be distributed to network nodes when they make blocks, with the amount cut in half every 4 years. [...]
> When that runs out, the system can support transaction fees if needed. It's based on open market competition, and there will probably always be nodes willing to process transactions for free. (Nakamoto, Bitcoin: A Peer-to-Peer Electronic Cash System 2008)

To be stable, the money supply needs to allow long-term investment, but also not allow intentional attacks by destruction.

In having an end capacity of just under 21 million Bitcoin (BCH), some Bitcoin will be "lost", but this is analogous to bullion money being lost. In time, it can be found, and returned into circulation. When a private key is lost, it is merely out of circulation. It may be many years, but all old addresses eventually become mineable and can be recovered.

Returning "lost" money into circulation is a future means of miner revenue and analogous to salvage firms who seek lost bullion on ships that have sunk in the sea.

To allow for this vision and end, the SV implementation of Bitcoin will be removing the flawed code that allows "burning" of coins permanently. This is not an instantaneous process, and it will take time, but this lost money will be returned into circulation. The full details will come before the changes.

OP_FALSE

OP_FALSE is an original OP_CODE that was designed to fail script paths in a predicate. It is used and needed, and has a range of uses, and in fact, it cannot (and should not) be disabled or removed.

The issue comes when a script is constructed to destroy Bitcoin. The aim in this is to remove value from Bitcoin and send it into an alternate system — it is a form of attack.

In Bitcoin, miners are the replacement for the various member banks in the U.S. Federal Reserve. The distinction is that the banks in the US Fed are incentivised to create more money. They act in collusion, that is social consensus.

Bitcoin alters this by making the miners—the equivalent of the member banks that set monetary policy—act in capitalist competition. This allows them to neither increase the money supply nor seek to subvert it. The miners ensure that the money supply is stable.

They do this by allowing the system to recover funds that are taken out of circulation.

Some parties have used OP_FALSE to issue a "proof-of-burn." This is what miners are aligned and incentivised to stop. Burning money by making it permanently un-spendable is an attack on

Bitcoin by those with a vested interest in creating something other than Bitcoin.

The aim was never to allow the creation of scripts that are designed to diminish the long-term viability of Bitcoin, and to this end miners will be able to recover this form of funds as if they were salvaging "sunken treasure." This returns the coins into circulation.

OP_RETURN

The OP_RETURN code is also used to create a lost-value transaction. The purpose of OP_RETURN is to make a marker, not to destroy Bitcoin. This will also be recoverable.

We will be publishing a strategy where OP_RETURNS are published on a time basis. The amount invested into the OP_RETURN will set the length of time before these are removed and pruned.

The result will be a message that remains for a set amount of time and then is prunable, returning the funds to miners through salvage and, after that, into circulation.

The exact details will be published later, but the concept would be to have OP_RETURN remain valid for a set length of time that is determined by the number of satoshis expended by the size of the data to be saved against the time in Unix time (that is, in seconds from when it is published).

This allows for both the use of OP_RETURN and a means to pay miners and archive nodes for delivering a service. This is not the final version, but for example:

- (V) number of satoshis (sent to miners in OP_RETURN) /
- (S) size of TX in KB =
- (T) time in 100 seconds, before the value is recoverable

$T = V / S$

So, if a 100-KB file is to be stored for 1 year, miners'

V = T*S = 31,536,000*100/100 = 0.315 BCH

The exact figures would be left to market forces to determine. When the time has expired, a sunk fee can then be recovered by miners.

Invalid OP_CODES (DSV, etc.)

If a transaction is intentionally sent to an invalid OP_Code such that it is burnt and removed from circulation, this again is just an attack against the total number of Bitcoins that can circulate, and it will be available for miners to recover.

The result is that those wanting to attack Bitcoin through a vain attempt to remove money from circulation and to extract it into a separate system (Tether, Omni, CounterParty, WHC, etc.) will find their attacks fail.

Bitcoin is resilient.

ENSURING STABILITY

Something people fail to understand about Bitcoin is that it is intentionally limited in what it can do and how it can be changed. This is purposeful. Bitcoin is designed to be stable money and for that reason it is not designed to have new opcodes added outside the need for a few security based replacements or to be altered. The very limited number of reserved words within Bitcoin are incredibly necessary. If these are wasted, the future of Bitcoin as a protocol is extremely limited. Some of these have already been wasted to implement time-based functions that could have been and have been enabled using nLockTime more efficiently.

The consequence is, if we want Bitcoin to remain and be a viable system that will last more than 20 years, we are down to two spare opcodes already. Of the total of 10 that are needed for hash and digital signature algorithms only eight remain.

SET IN STONE AS OF VERSION 0.1.0

This is a part of what this means. The design of Bitcoin is not to create an idealised socialist utopia, it is to create stable global money. To do this, it is required that we have a system that does not change without reason. We have already seen this being subverted by developers. The idea at present is to experiment first by adding bells and whistles and hope for the best. This may be the way that many applications work within Silicon Valley, but it is not how money works, and this is one of the key problems right now.

In Bitcoin Cash, we had the foolish attempt to mindlessly add additional opcodes and the reason was that this would bring traffic. It is exactly the opposite of what is needed. Financial organisations and even the idea of a listed ETF derived from stability. Right now, this is the one thing Bitcoin fails to exhibit as people constantly try to change it.

The reasons for reserved opcodes should be clear. They are necessary to create a script system that is stable and can be used as a financial system. To do this, we need to be able to create contracts that can last not one, or five, or even 10 years. There are financial instruments that last over 100 years. If Bitcoin is money, it must be able to handle these and that requires stability.

With the existing script code fully re-enabled, there is nothing that could be conceivably desired that cannot be done within Bitcoin. The lack of vision of one developer does not require that the entire system and protocol is changed.

Bitcoin needs to be a stable system to be money. We have invested in hash power and intend to use that for the sole goal of scaling and stabilising Bitcoin.

When you are told that we need to develop to integrate to grow, the reality is that this is about scaling the existing Bitcoin protocol and developing on top of that protocol. Bitcoin is an economic system it is not designed to be altered frequently.

Unfortunately, there are many things in Bitcoin that have been added and must now remain. P2SH is one of these horrible kludges. These cannot ever be removed. This is not the same as making a bad script and losing a little of your own funds. Any additions to the protocol we have just noted are permanent. Bitcoin cannot ever be altered to reverse these changes.

The atomic structure of Gold is defined.

If you add or remove a proton, it is no longer gold. Some changes (P2SH) are analogous in Bitcoin to adding a neutron to gold, it can be done, but the resulting system is less stable.

It is time to start moving away from the idea that Bitcoin is broken and to start scaling it and allowing it to become what it was designed to be — stable money.

THE ROAD AHEAD

Right now, disk storage doubles each year in capacity. CPU power doubles each 18 months. Fibre speeds and capacity double each 9 months. (Gilder 1996)

This is exponential growth on a wide scale. This is the type of technological change that economists call disruptive change. There is not a visionary on Earth who can forecast what this will truly mean in 20 years. Even 10 years is astounding. Just take some of the figures that this leads to by 2020:
- Hard disk drives (likely memory-based and at phenomenal speeds and with low-power sleep states that provide an instant start capacity).
- Two (2) Petabytes of storage in a personal device.
- CPU speeds of 100 times those we have now.
- Wireless network bandwidth of 100 Gigabytes/Sec or mere.

This means that we can expect low power Internet tablets for less than $1. These will be able to make free VoIP calls. Anywhere to anywhere.

This is a world where in just 9 years, nearly everything will go online. I have already noted how FMCGs will have IP addresses and that even light globes are going online. The future is one where a simple embedded Linux controller will cost less than a cent for 100 devices.

The digital divide is changing. Right now, only the rich nations have the necessary levels of access to the Internet and ecommerce. The future is one where even the poorest countries will have complete access.

Think what this means for forensics. For privacy (or the end of.)

Start to think what this means for politics. In 10 years, we will have low-cost tablets. These will be disposable, thin, and easy to hide with access to the Internet. This is anywhere, anytime. This will even mean access in places such as North Korea where Internet access is extremely restricted.

You may say that this will still pose an issue.

After all, the levels of literacy in many developing nations is low. Here is the rub, applications that talk to you are already available. SIRI is not new. I have been using Dragon Voice type for a decade now, but it is a CPU hog. Well, that is changing, and these systems are improving. Further, I have "RealVoices" that offer a truly human sounding voice from the PC.

In 2020, we will have a future when any person, anyplace on Earth, can talk to any other person. This is instant translation of over 100 languages to any other. Of seeing text displayed on screen in any language from any language.

These are not idle claims, they are existing technologies that right now take large systems, but which in time (only a few years) will run on a device smaller than a watch.

Even a nation as isolated and as poor as North Korea will see radical changes. Ask yourself what these device costs lead to. Think of the pamphlet drops we have seen in the past. In the future, it will cost less than it does to drop a piece of paper to drop a set of digital devices on a village.

Tablets that seem as if magic to the people who have been isolated from technology so long. Devices that will open the world, politics, and learning to the poorest peoples on Earth.

Just imagine for a moment

Let your mind wander. For even with all I am saying, there is nothing I can state that will cover the changes, the fundamental differences that will develop from this by 2030. We are entering a new Era, a new world. There is no way to change this fact now, we have already passed the point of no return.

Imagine for a moment in the coming years that you are that poor villager or peasant in North Korea. You have been isolated for your entire life. You have seen and heard little with only the doubts and false knowledge provided by your "leader."

Now, suddenly a device is dropped in a crate from an airborne mission. Far too many at once for even a totalitarian regime to stop.

This device talks to you in your own language. It answers questions. It provides knowledge freely. It shows pictures and videos. Anything you ask. You can see news; you can listen to speeches from the UN or movie stars in your own language. instantly translated.

You can access a wealth of classic books and if you cannot read these will be translated and read to you in your native dialect.

ON EDUCATION

Think for a moment what this will be regarding education. The existing school and University systems will be exposed to increasing competition. Not local competition any longer, but International. The best teachers will be able to teach from anywhere. I already have students in multiple countries.

In time, we will choose not from a small list of subjects offered in a local high school, but from a global collection and wealth of knowledge that is beyond my ability to contemplate fully. It is beyond any individual's power to truly grasp.

ADD HOLOGRAPHIC TECHNOLOGY

Right now, personal projection technology is expensive, power hungry, and available only to the rich. There are already companies creating virtual board rooms where the members are projected into a room they do not inhabit at the time. This is a 2.5-dimensional effect right now. A decade will change this. It will also make it simple and inexpensive. In the coming decade, projection devices will be a simple feature in phones. There are some already in development with this technology.

This is just a taste. I will write more on this topic. We must start thinking and planning now for the future is coming. What we make of it will depend on how we act now. A decade is a very short time.

THE BSV ROAPDMAP

The goal of Bitcoin is to be cash, but there is only one way to achieve this. Bitcoin must be a commodity ledger. To be money, Bitcoin cannot be a speculative gambling asset. For many, this short-term zero-sum game and "get-rich-fast Ponzi" are all Bitcoin means. To them, Bitcoin is all about HODL and the false idea that money and value come from simple scarcity.

If scarcity alone made something valuable, then many unwanted things would be collected and exchanged. An example is an old Telex. This obsolete technology is extremely hard to find now, and yet it remains worthless. Value does not come from scarcity, rather scarcity allows things that are in demand to be traded at the margin.

For money to have value as cash, it needs to be more than a simple speculative asset. That is, as cash, Bitcoin is not simply a tool to gamble with.

We are accelerating growth and looking at real uses of the Bitcoin ledger. As a commodity ledger, Bitcoin has value outside of speculative gambling and market guessing. It has value to a business seeking a stable and secure ledger. More, contracts can be created on the platform that allow businesses to integrate other services.

In testing, we have already achieved block sizes of over a gigabyte. This is far from the end. In the next 6 months we will scale our systems and propagation limits to allow the propagation of transactions at a rate exceeding 2,500 TPS (transactions per second.)

A block cap of 512 MB is equal to a sustained transaction rate of 2,000 TPS (settled.) This processing level exceeds the combined peak rates for Ripple (XRP), Ethereum (ETH), Bitcoin Core(BTC), and all other cryptocurrencies combined with the transactional ability of PayPal. The claim of Ripple in the LAB of 1,500 settlement exchanges (and not real transactions/sec) coupled with the real sustained 175 TPS of XRP's reality shows just how important this is.

The 12-month goal of an ability for handling sustained 2.0-GB blocks allows a combined transaction rate of 8,000 TPS settled and allows handling up to Visa-level transaction volumes. Not what they do in a lab, but the real world.

With Tokenized as a secure platform for issuing securities that can be legally registered with bank-issued digital fiat on Bitcoin, we would be able to have all debit-card and other payment traffic on our chain for less than Visa or MasterCard can do.

Past this, we are looking to 1-TB blocks and no limits.

Welcome to the future of finance.

Going forward we will start to open up, and to allow business use of the Bitcoin blockchain. Bitcoin scales. In the coming years, we plan to support an unbounded block size and as many transactions as people are willing to send us.

BUSINESS USE

To many in the "crypto" space the entire use of Bitcoin and alternative chains has been as a speculative asset. We are going to start to show a long-term path for miners, not exchanges and speculators, but those seeking to build the next-generation Internet of value.

The Bitcoin blockchain is a commodity ledger. It is a method to exchange value without the issue of double spending that has plagued all other attempts to create a digital currency. The fallacy is seeing Bitcoin as a road to short-term riches. The long-term road is pathed using commercial transactions.

Here, it is not the value of the coin that matters; in fact, if the value of Bitcoin is volatile, it does nothing to the use of Bitcoin as a commodity ledger. At scale, we expect the cost to a merchant for sending a simple marker and record transaction securely encoded to remain under $0.001 USD. Over time, this will be lower.

A more complex contract could be encoded for $0.05 USD.

The fact of all this is that it does not matter whether the merchant seeks to pay in USD, GBP, or Yuan. They are not seeking use as a purely speculation-based system, so the market of the transaction is sold as a commodity in their local currency.

We have already documented several 100s of inventions that have real-world value today. These are concepts and seeds of businesses that we will provide to developers seeking to extend the Bitcoin protocol on SV — not to take down the state or anything along those lines, but simple and boring uses such as technological data plumbing. This will be tax invoices and contract-exchange platforms — systems that allow a user to purchase an item in the local store and have it recorded and available later for use as a tax record. It could even be automated to load into an accounting system.

The concepts for inventions in our portfolios and the associated inventions will be available to open the use of the Bitcoin blockchain globally.

These records would be stored in the public blockchain in a completely private manner and without loss. A miner will be paid for processing the transactions, and the merchant and user now have a system that can minimise fraud, loss, and alteration.

The reality is that an exchange would be able to occur for a cost lower than existing paper-based invoice and receipt systems.

Most importantly, as the cost is paid as it is used, the system is not subject to volatility. Merchants would pay in their local currency and not care if the transaction was more or less expensive in Bitcoin to USD terms. The number of Bitcoins required will fluctuate, but the costs to the merchant would be stable.

So, what do we see as our market? The crypto community?

No, we see our market as the world. Any merchant in any country. We plan to open development of systems that will have billions of people using Bitcoin in the coming years, without even knowing that they are using Bitcoin. Basically, we seek to create a system that proves the ends which reflect how any good system should be — not one based on ideology and religious drive, but simple efficiency and value.

Interestingly, even with a dispute as we see today between ABC and SV no loss of transactions would have occurred on the SV chain. Our solutions and businesses deploying these would not even have to concern themselves with the ongoing "hash war."

The system is that resilient.

INSTANT TRANSACTIONS

The "FUD" around Bitcoin is deep, but we shall start to clear it up.

The truth is, most things in Bitcoin are simple. Many in the industry try to tell you otherwise. They seek to gain a falsely earnt place as the "High Priests of crypto." They also seek to manipulate markets with false claims of vulnerabilities that do not exist — a form of fraud.

We had the lie and scam claim of Selfish Mining for years. That was the lie of the land for a long time. It was claimed that Bitcoin needed to be fixed by these disingenuous scammers, who really wanted nothing more than to ensure Bitcoin would not scale. Now, the false narrative, the lie, is the "0-conf-is-not-safe" mantra.

The latest is the fraudulent and unscientific claim of being able to double spend Bitcoin, that they could get away with a fraud and steal from a merchant that has taken an unconfirmed transaction and walk out with the ill-gotten goods. As always, they do a test in a lab with no relation to reality, but that is not even the start of it.

What is "0-conf" or an instant transaction?

To start to define any so-called attack, we need to start by defining what a 0-conf or an instant transaction is. The so-called attack is only of concern in a scenario where a merchant and client seek to complete and exchange in moments. That is, the client seeks to pay and then to "bounce" a transaction in seconds by fraudulently replacing it with another transaction that spends the same input transaction to a separate output.

The claim is that this can defraud the merchant, and thus a double spend means that the merchant is not safe.

The truth is, this is an equivocation made by those seeking to falsely manipulate markets; it is a form of fraud. The fraud is the claim of a double spend. The truth is, these do not exist. Anonymous accounts are always used in making these claims. The key point is to appear valid and scientific to those without the skills to see the truth, and really, to deliver a message:

- including false or deceptive messages, and
- leaving out important information.

The reality is that all transactions have risk, but to minimise risk, you need to act in a certain way.

For a merchant, this means not assuming you can send a transaction without a suitable mining fee. Note that, again, the merchant sends. This is the first and most critical part of all this. Bitcoin is a peer-to-peer system. It is the exchange of messages (transactions) that forms the peer component of the system, not mining. Mining is there to ensure the creation of a competitive system to stop double spending.

- Users exchange peer-to-peer with the ability to have messages sent to another party (through the miners) to be collected later when they log into their wallet.
- Miners are paid to not only verify transactions, but to find errors in the efforts of other miners, and to invalidate these.

So, for a merchant—a vending machine even—to take a risk and accept a transaction from a client, they need to do this in a manner that makes the risk worthwhile. This is just a fact of life. It is nothing to be concerned with. Like all other aspects of life; it means doing things correctly.

The following process is how a merchant process should be handled; this is what a 0-conf attack will need to overcome to be a real attack and not a marketing fraud.

Step 1. The client makes an offer to the merchant. This can be a request for a coffee in a café or selecting a product in a vending machine, whatever.

Step 2. The merchant sets the value and exchange rate, and hands a template to the client. This is a Bitcoin-transaction template with an output address, any conditions and the required scripts, and payment terms.

Step 3. The reality is that the merchant sets the invoice up, and exchanges this with the client. We are also not talking about complex redemption systems.

Rather, we are allowing the merchant and client to exchange a transaction template using an SPV wallet.

The part that few seem to have understood is that keys should not be reused.

If we take the linked process, we can start with a known or determinable public key (even one on a CA on a PKI system) that is never used. From this, there are methods to create a series of output addresses that are designed to be used once and only once.

In the case of the merchant, we can have a system that allows all output addresses to be linked from a privacy-based scenario and yet to also be verifiably demonstrable from an audit and business scenario. That is, shareholders and even tax officials could determine that the invoice was not split or padded and that the correct amounts had been allocated to the correct addresses.

So, you can prove a private ledger created as a sub-set of the Bitcoin blockchain and remain private.

This seems to be a difficult concept for some people. In the real world, a merchant or vendor gives you an invoice to pay. This does not change in the Bitcoin world. You send what is requested. The crypto-anarchist set seems to have this idea of what Bitcoin is, where a user can dictate how a merchant does business. Sorry, this is reality.

The merchant creates a template that is handed to the user.

Step 4. With the merchant's template, the user can now decide on what input coins they want to use and where their outputs (if any) will go.

The user accepts the template, adds the input coins and sets the change address. Output 3 is not a "real" output as it is a miner fee. It is the MINIMUM amount that the user needs to send such that the total fees are paid to the miner and that there is a sufficient additional amount (not specified in output) that is now set as a fee for miners.

It can even be compressed into a human-displayable format (one of the many aspects of what we have as Metanet) that is signed. To make this more private (in certain legal industries), a merchant could add inputs, and the client could add outputs to themselves (to make tracing more private).

The signed transaction is handed to the merchant. In this example, the merchant has set a requirement for 0.50 units in mining fees. If the client hands the merchant a transaction using less than this, they will reject it. It is the merchant and not the user who sets the terms used here, and the merchant can simply not allow the sale, if it is under the offer price.

In this example of a template, the merchant has a minimum output of 12.5 units with an optional field for tips. The merchant could automate the fees used in the template so that the client pays more as they add more input transactions, if this was desired. With SV, we do not see input transactions as a concern. These inputs lower the UTXO size, so miners should be willing to accept large input sets and charge based on the outputs (which was in the initial template exchange). It is one thing we want to push in SV.

The fees cover mining and VAT and leave enough to pay the mining fee. If the client sends a lower value transaction to the miner, then the merchant will not have to accept it. Even if the user was a particularly stupid one, and thought they can do something to fool the merchant, such as sending the signed template, rather than returning it to the merchant, well, then they have legally made a donation to the merchant and not engaged in a legal contract to supply.

The merchant can (at their leisure) return funds to the client (with a handling fee), or have the client sit in a corner and wait until the fee has cleared (one confirm or multiple confirmations), or require that the client pay again and state that they (the merchant) will return funds (minus a mining fee and any handling charge) to the client after the transaction has cleared with 6 confirmations and the initial invoice is paid.

It is how the real world works. Bitcoin is not about allowing users to tell businesses how to operate. If you have such an idea, you are deluded.

Step 5. With the signed transaction returned from the client, the merchant now starts by sending a request to the mempool of the miners (or their own, if they are large enough to warrant having one;

and for a franchise or group, this could be a company system) to check the inputs.
1. The merchant checks the input TXs (transactions) and makes certain that these have not been spent. They do this by randomly polling miners (remember, only miners are nodes in Bitcoin).
2. The merchant ensures that the transaction from the user matches the template and that it includes enough fees and the total is at least the minimum (if the user wants to donate more to miners, who are we to stop them.)
3. The merchant sends the transaction to multiple mining nodes, and relays simultaneously.
4. The merchant rechecks the transaction inputs with miners, after sending their signed payment.

If the merchant detects a double spend, it is a fraud. The merchant has the legal right to detain the client in many countries and have the authorities take them off, just as is the case with shoplifters right now. This is before the client even received the goods. They can at this point be legally arrested for a larceny, and it is the same as when a person has attempted to pass a bad cheque.

The definition and use of cheques are covered by The Bills of Exchange Act 1882, and the Cheques Acts of 1957 and 1992. The most recent amendment to the Bills of Exchange Act occurred via the Small Business, Enterprise and Employment Act, which gained Royal Assent in 2015, eliminating the need for cheques to be physically transported around the country (and this definition incorporates a Bitcoin transaction that has not been confirmed).

In the U.S., there are state laws for this—these vary, but are generally similar to this one.

Step 6. The merchant now provides the goods to the client. They have checked twice, made certain that the inputs had not been spent, and then they are safe in the assumption that the miners have received the transaction and no fraud has been attempted.

That is all there is. It is not some technical system of fraud proofs and the anarchist utopia that no state will exist. Bitcoin works inside and with the law.

If the merchant sets the template, pays the mining fees, and sends the transaction, there is no measurable risk of a double spend. Just as merchants will not allow customers to set payment terms and require a cheque from a strange country to just be used in consideration, they will not allow payment under strange terms.

The reality is that in 2 seconds (or less) the merchant has checked the transaction, and the reality is that you do not get to send a double spend. A double-spend attack is not about replacing your own transaction, it is about defrauding a merchant who allows small-value instant transactions. If the merchant sends, the chance of sending to all miners and getting a system that has a probabilistic chance of a free coffee are small. If the miners are polled after the send, the reality is that you will be caught double spending and get away with this fraud less than once in 100 billion times. In checking more miners, the merchant can be even more well assured.

The truth is, if you try and double spend, you will see a set of flashing lights and not even have the chance to smell the coffee.

If you are Amazon, even this is not needed. The online merchant simply stops delivery as soon as they find the fraud attempt. Say you send an order with Amazon; then, the store starts to process the order. It is likely going to be hours before the invoice is touched, and if the transaction was "double-spent," you have signed evidence of fraud and simply do not pack the goods.

THE LONG-HAUL

Many people in the "crypto currency exchange" industry want to see me gone. They accuse me of contradicting myself. Life can be complex. Contradictions exist because humans are messy. There is a quote by Ayn Rand that I like even though it's not technically correct:

> "Contradictions do not exist. Whenever you think you are facing a contradiction, check your premises. You will find that one of them is wrong."

In maths, we know that this is correct. But the world is not mathematics and people are not rational. That stated, whenever a contradiction does exist, we know that we do need to check our premises. What we find is that there is something amiss.

What I'd like you to think about is very simple. I am being painted as a fraud and a criminal by people who opposed me and my ideals. My ideals involve delivering an immutable evidence chain that will record transactions and make fraud difficult. On the other hand, we have people who promote anarchy and crime.

Let's have a look at some of the key detractors. Greg Maxwell was involved in anti-sec and helped with the theft of thousands of copyrighted documents and other intellectual property. He broke into computer systems and altered records and released this stolen information to the world. Yet he calls for me to be imprisoned as he claims I altered records.

Roger Ver is seeking to create dark web markets and was an early promoter and proponent of Silk Road. He was imprisoned for selling explosives and for fraudulently signing a declaration stating that these were not explosives amongst other things. He is promoting systems that will allow anarchy, drug markets, assassination markets, and crime generally. Yet he calls me a fraud.

Vitelik Butheran has been behind the creation of the biggest Ponzi market and scheme this decade with ICOs that have extracted billions of dollars from unwary individuals. These were created with the sole purpose of allowing people to bypass regulatory control and to extract money from individuals who would not be allowed to generally trade as they are uninformed and unsophisticated investors. Vitelik calls this democratising finance, generally a term used when people seek to dupe the uninformed. He calls BSV a scam as we seek to work within the government and regulatory controls.

CZ of Binance and individuals associated with him run one of the biggest money-laundering operations in the public world and seek to allow individuals to easily launder money using crypto currency. He calls me a fraud because I seek to add Know Your Customer and anti-money laundering requirements to bitcoin and other exchanges.

Effectively, these people call me a fraud because I'm willing to work within a regulatory framework. All these people opposing me seek a system that allows drug markets and crime.

What is interesting is that all these individuals and practically everyone opposing me seeks to create a system that allows illegal activities to occur with impunity. I'm seeking a system that works within the justice system and law. Which one seems more likely to be the fraud?

Unfortunately for them, I'm not going anywhere. Not now. Not in the next decade. Not in the next 20 years. You see, I'm here to stay.

What people fail to understand is that I do not write patents covering Bitcoin. What (IP) we give away on BSV is protected by patents that equally apply to any other system, but are no longer close to being free. The distinction is that other systems will need to pay. By the end of this year I hope that we will have around 1,000 patents published. More importantly, the initial patent families should place us in advance of any other player in the industry. You see, we don't publish straightaway. Others do, but we don't because that would give away what we're doing.

So, while a few industry players are trying to learn how to swim in this pond and inventing single-use limited patents and intellectual property we create new technology that will radically change everything.

In fact, I see some of the patents that we're developing leading to thousands of applications each.

So, the truth of the matter is that I am not going anywhere.

I won't be out of this industry in 20 years' time. You see I don't intend to retire. You have no idea how much we have been doing in the background. In a couple years' time we will have a system that can take the entire world's global commerce and every other blockchain and run it without missing a heartbeat. More importantly, we have ways to stop all the not-so-fun systems, the scams in the bucket shops. I expect them to cry, to call foul, to do anything in their power to stop me. The fact is that they missed their opportunity. Bitcoin is here to stay. Real Bitcoin, not the temporary fraudulent system that people try and call Bitcoin (BTC) but Bitcoin. You see, Bitcoin is a stable protocol. If you change the protocol, you change it from being Bitcoin.

Please bet against me.

If you are someone like a Binance supporter, please bet every cent you have, and add leverage with all that you can possibly get and bet more. I want you to, because I want you to be begging on the streets with all the criminals that are going to be out of jobs. I want you to learn, criminality does not pay.

> *If you trust in yourself ... and believe in your dreams ... and follow your star ... you'll still get beaten by people who spent their time working hard and learning things and weren't so lazy.*
>
> Terry Pratchett, *The Wee Free Men*

ACKNOWLEDGEMENTS

Where possible, acknowledgement and credit has been given in context. Additional thanks to Medium.com users Will Devine, Joel Dalais, Ben E, Jerry David, wer5lcy, tonesnotes, Ryan X. Charles, Alex Fauvel, Roger Taylor, gabriel, and Lin Zheming.

REFERENCES:

Dodd, N. 1994. *The Sociology of Money*. Cambridge: Polity.
More, T. 1516. *Utopia*.
Plato. 1961. *The Collected Dialogues of Plato*, ed. E. Hamilton and H. Cairns. Princeton, NJ: Princeton University Press.
Proudhon, J.-F. 1927. *Proudhon's Solution of the Social Problem*. New York: Vanguard Press.
Ruskin, J. 1862. "Unto This Last" *Cornhill Magazine*.
Simmel, G. 2004. *The Philosophy of Money*. London: Routledge.
Smith, L.D. 1997. *The Law of Tracing*. Oxford.

BIBLIOGRAPHY

2018. *Bitcoin Wiki*. 26 Jan. https://en.Bitcoin.it/wiki/Coinbase.

Bitcoin.com. 2018. "Interview with Clemens Ley, CTO of Yours.org | Satoshi's Vision Conference, Tokyo 2018." *YouTube.* 4 Apr. https://www.youtube.com/watch?v=AY0b7zDvjbo.

Black, Henry Campbell. 1995. *A Law Dictionary Containing Definitions of the Terms and Phrases of American and English Jurisprudence, Ancient and Modern.* The Lawbook Exchange, Ltd.

Bollen, Rhys. 2013. *The Legal Status of Online Currencies: Are Bitcoin the Future?* , (2013) 24 JBFLP 272 at 275. Available at SSRN: https://ssrn.com/abstract=2285247, Monash University - Faculty of Law.

Carnegie, Andrew. 1901. *The Gospel of Wealth and Other Timely Essays.* Century Company.

Clinch, Matt. 2013. "Bitcoin recognized by Germany as 'private money'." *CNBC.com.* 19 August. https://www.cnbc.com/id/100971898.

2019. "Contract Definition." *Bitcoin Wiki.* 25 February. https://en.bitcoin.it/wiki/Contract.

Daily, Cindy. 2018. "BCH Smart Contract Is Coming----Wormhole Protocol Proposed by Bitmain Developers(Part Two)." *Yours.* https://www.yours.org/content/bch-smart-contract-is-coming----wormhole-protocol-proposed-by-bitmain-6c353fe1b515.

Froomkin, Michael. 1997. "The Unintended Consequences of eCash." A position paper by Michael Froomkin for the Panel on 'Governmental and Social Implications of Digital Money', Burlingame, CA.

Gilder, George. 1996. *Telecosm: How Infinite Bandwidth Will Revolutionize Our World.* American Heritage Custom Publishing.

Nakamoto, Satoshi. 2009. "Bitcoin open source implementation of P2P currency." *P2P Foundation.* 11 Feb.

http://p2pfoundation.ning.com/forum/topics/bitcoin-open-source.

—. 2008. "Bitcoin: A Peer-to-Peer Electronic Cash System." *Bitcoin.org.* https://bitcoin.org/bitcoin.pdf.

Newman, M. E., and D J Watts. 1999. *Scaling and percolation in the small-world network model.* E 60, 7332, Phys. Rev, E 60, 7332.

Olfati-Saber, Reza. 2005. "Ultrafast Consensus in Small-World Networks." *Caltech.* 10 June. https://authors.library.caltech.edu/5147/1/OLFacc05.pdf.

Rees, D. 1988. *Lectures on the Asymptotic Theory of Ideals (London Mathematical Society Lecture Note Series).* Cambridge: Cambridge University Press.

The New York Times. 1958. "Peter J. M'Coy, 70, Former U.S. Aide." 19 July.

Travelex Limited v Commissioner of Taxation. 2008. 1961 (FCA).

United States v. Sanders. 1988. 696 F. Supp. 327 (U.S. District Court for the Northern District of Illinois).

Watterson, Tom, and Todd Zerega. 2013. "Regulating Bitcoins: CFTC vs. SEC?" *The Swap Report.* 31 Dec. https://www.theswapreport.com/2013/12/articles/general/regulating-bitcoins-cftc-vs-sec/.

Wright, Craig S. 2008. "The Impact of Internet Intermediary Liability ." *SSRN.* 17 April. https://ssrn.com/abstract=2953929.

About the Author

Craig Wright is a computer scientist, businessman, and inventor. As the creator of Bitcoin under the pseudonym Satoshi Nakamoto, he inspired the world with a vision of electronic cash and commodity money, while introducing the idea of blockchain as a transformative technology platform.

Currently, Dr. Wright is Chief Scientist for nChain – the global leader in advisory, research, and development of blockchain technologies. nChain focuses on igniting massive growth and adoption of the original Bitcoin design, protocol, and vision, in the form of Bitcoin Satoshi Vision (BSV).

A prolific researcher, Dr. Wright has been a lecturer and researcher in computer science at Charles Sturt University. He has also authored many articles, academic papers, and books on IT, security, Bitcoin, and other cryptocurrency issues. Dr. Wright is now a sought-after public speaker internationally on security, Bitcoin, and cryptocurrency topics, while also presenting his research findings at academic and business conferences.

Dr. Wright has numerous advanced academic degrees in diverse fields, including a Doctor of Philosophy (PhD) degree in Computer Science and Economics from Charles Sturt University, a Doctor of Theology (ThD) degree from United Theological College awarded in 2003, a master's degree in Statistics, and a master's degree in International Commercial Law. Dr. Wright is currently a candidate for two additional PhDs: in Law at Leicester University in the United Kingdom and Applied Mathematics at CNAM in Paris, France.

Follow Dr Wright at http://craigwright.net
Learn more about Bitcoin SV at https://bitcoinsv.io/

From Paul Democritou

Fact: "By the time you've finished reading *The Crypto Factor*, you'll know more about how to succeed in the cryptosphere than 98 percent of so-called investing gurus - guaranteed!"

Do you want to learn from the most respected and successful global influencers?

Do you want to discover the mindset of the greats? To learn how you can achieve financial freedom while avoiding the dangers and pitfalls of crypto?

Get your copy of The Crypto Factor now, and join the crypto revolution today

https://books2read.com/u/4AJQgN

COMING SOON

"With even more explosive insider Interviews and secrets from Crypto's top talent."

The Crypto Factor

Need to know what's happening on the blockchain?

But don't have the time to keep track of industry "news" sites?

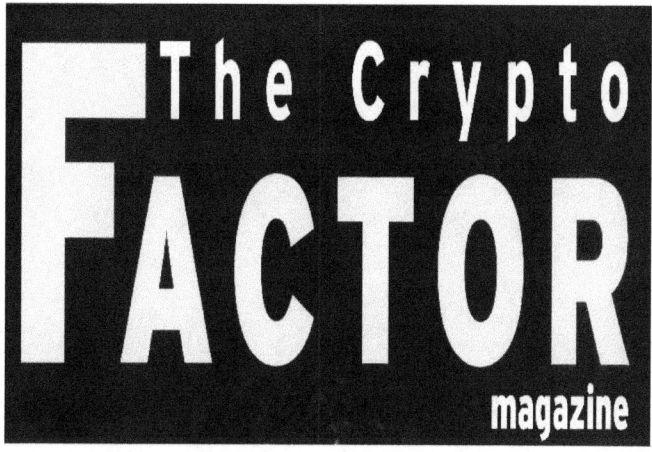

Subscribe to The Crypto Factor magazine today and get 3 issues FREE

https://TheCryptoFactor.subscribemenow.com

www.ingramcontent.com/pod-product-compliance
Lightning Source LLC
Chambersburg PA
CBHW070639220526
45466CB00001B/232